CANOEING THE DELAWARE RIVER

Gary Letcher

Rutgers University Press
New Brunswick, New Jersey

CANOEING THE DELAWARE RIVER

A Guide to the River and Shore

Second Paperback Printing, 1990

Library of Congress Cataloging in Publication Data

Letcher, Gary, 1952–
  Canoeing the Delaware River.

  Bibliography: p.
  1. Canoes and canoeing—Delaware River (N.Y.-Del.
and N.J.)—Guide-books. 2. Delaware River (N.Y.-Del.
and N.J.)—Description and travel—Guide-books. 3. Canoes
and canoeing—Pennsylvania—Guide-books. 4. Pennsylvania—
Description and travel—1981–   —Guide-books.
I. Title
GV776.D34L47   1984   797.1′22′09749   84-13434
ISBN 0-8135-1076-7
ISBN 0-8135-1077-5 (pbk.)

This book is dedicated to those with whom I have paddled the Delaware: my wife, Shirley; my parents, William and Sherry Letcher; my sisters, Donna and Roxanne; my friends, Stu Gillard, Bill Goldfarb, Dave Griffin, Illse Heacox, Zev Kaplan, Courtenay Kling, Gary Lesslie, Rich Messina, Sal Misuraca, Greg Pulis, Joan Snyder, and Jane and Steve Wenner.

Contents

Acknowledgments

This book would not have been possible without the generous assistance of the following people: Mary Ann Butler, Port Jervis/ Tri-State Chamber of Commerce; C. R. Fauber, Interpretive Specialist, Delaware Water Gap National Recreation Area; Ruth Jones, Kittatinny Canoes; Rick Landers, Bob and Rick Landers' Canoes; Barry Leilich, Chief Naturalist, New Jersey State Park Service; Sam McBrian, Point Pleasant Canoes; J. Wallis Perry, Pike County Historical Society; Paul Peterson, Chief Engineer, Delaware River Joint Toll Bridge Commission; Ted Day, Regional Engineer, New York Department of Transportation; John Skiba, New York Geological Survey; Paul Stern, Superintendent, Delaware and Raritan Canal State Park; Dawes Thompson, Public Information Officer, Delaware River Basin Commission; Carney Umphreys, Pennsylvania Geological Survey; and Gretchen Wrenshall, Administrative Assistant to the Mayor, Easton, Pennsylvania. I would also like to acknowledge Angela and Greg Pulis, and David and Beth Griffin, who assisted with the logging of riverside services; Stu Gillard, who aided in aerial reconnaissance and photos; and Shirley Letcher, who sketched the maps.

Special thanks to Pam Harris-Hill, of Anchorage, Alaska, who spent many weekend and evening hours preparing the manuscript.

I am indebted as well to the following sources: Herbert C. Kraft, *The Archeology of the Tocks Island Area* for my discussion of Indian artifacts; William F. Henn, *Life Along the Dela-*

ware from Bushkill to Milford (pp. 89–111) for my account of the old bridges at Dingmans Ferry and his *Westfall Township, Gateway to the West* (pp. 37, 24, 78) for information on Mapes Ferry in Port Jervis, the tale of Sally Decker and her brother, and Dingmans Ferry; Charles Hine, *The Old Mine Road* (pp. 157–158, 153–154, 5–9) for the incident of Moses Van Campen and the Indian, the origin of the name of Walpack Township, and the history of the Old Mine Road; J. Wallace Hoff, *Two Hundred Miles on the Delaware* (pp. 48, 70, 76, 148) for his descriptions of Narrowsburg, the Roebling Bridge at Lackawaxen, the Delaware and Hudson Canal, and Ringing Rocks. The accounts of the New York and Erie Railroad, the nineteenth-century rafting industry, and the Walking Purchase have drawn on the following works respectively: Edward Hungerford, *Men of Erie* (pp. 78–81); Harry B. Weiss, *Rafting on the Delaware River* (p. 21); Clinton Alfred Weslager, *The Delaware Indians* (pp. 188–191).

CANOEING THE DELAWARE RIVER

Introduction

THE PLAN OF THE BOOK

This book is divided into ten river sections. Each division begins with a general introduction to that part of the river followed by a descriptive mile-by-mile river guide with recreational maps. A features section usually follows next, elaborating on points of special interest. An account of camping and other services concludes each section. The appendix, complete with river mileages, provides a quick guide to the Delaware and its public access areas, its rapids, its geological, historical, cultural, and recreational highlights. Together the appendix and the headings within the chapters offer the reader a ready means of locating points of special interest. Finally, the novice canoeist can locate unfamiliar canoeing terms in the glossary at the back of the book.

Each section can be canoed in one day and corresponds to a series of recreational maps available from the Delaware River Basin Commission (DRBC). The DRBC first published its maps in 1964 and issued a revised series in 1979. The original maps classified rapids on a scale from I to VI, but this scale was unrelated to the International Scale of River Difficulty developed by the American White Water Association. Following the old DRBC maps, a canoeist could conceivably navigate with ease a rapid marked as Class IV, only to believe mistakenly that he could paddle safely through a Class IV rapid on another river. Until the 1979 DRBC maps corrected this problem, the standards for

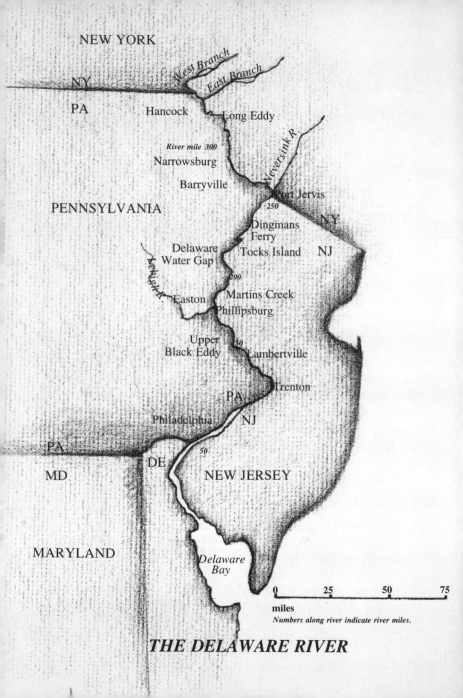

NEW YORK

NY

PA

West Branch

East Branch

Hancock

Long Eddy

Neversink R.

River mile 300

Narrowsburg

Barryville

Port Jervis

250

PENNSYLVANIA

NY

Dingmans
Ferry

NJ

Delaware
Water Gap

Tocks Island

Lehigh R.

200

Easton

Martins Creek

Phillipsburg

Upper
Black Eddy

50

Lambertville

Trenton

PA

Philadelphia

NJ

PA

MD

DE

50

NEW JERSEY

MARYLAND

*Delaware
Bay*

0   25   50   75

miles

Numbers along river indicate river miles.

THE DELAWARE RIVER

classification were entirely different. The Delaware River is now graded according to the International Scale of River Difficulty, which follows:

Class I—Moving water with a few riffles and small waves. Few or no obstructions.

Class II—Easy rapids with waves up to three feet and wide, clear channels that are obvious without scouting. Some maneuvering required.

Class III—Rapids with high, irregular waves capable of swamping an open canoe. Narrow passages that often require complex maneuvering. May require scouting from shore.

Class IV—Long, difficult rapids with constricted passages that require precise maneuvering in very turbulent waters. Scouting from shore necessary; conditions make rescue difficult. *Generally not possible for open canoes*. Boaters in covered canoes and kayaks should have ability to eskimo roll.

Class V—Extremely difficult, long, and very violent rapids with highly congested routes, which should always be scouted from shore. Rescue conditions difficult. Significant hazard to life in the event of a mishap. Ability to eskimo roll essential for boaters in kayaks and decked canoes.

Class VI—Very dangerous, nearly impossible to navigate. For teams of experts only, after a close study has been made and all precautions taken.

There are no Class IV, Class V, or Class VI rapids on the Delaware River. Under normal conditions, only Wells Falls at Lambertville is rated above Class II. In high water, Skinners Falls (above Narrowsburg), Shohola Rift (below Barryville), Foul Rift (below Belvidere), and Wells Falls might all be considered Class III. This book, in conformity with the 1979 DRBC maps, uses the International Scale of River Difficulty.

The water level of the Delaware River fluctuates widely between spring floods and summer droughts. The accounts in the river guides of this book are based on the moderate flow typical of June, July, and August. Higher or lower flow might change dramatically the characteristics of rapids, and this is noted to the extent possible. During the high cold flows of April, May, and early June, most Delaware rapids should be regarded as one class higher than indicated by this book and the DRBC maps. When flooding occurs, the river is too dangerous to canoe, regardless of the time of year.

The mileage indicated on each river guide and recreational map corresponds to the 1979 DRBC maps and is measured from the mouth of the river at Delaware Bay. There are no actual mileposts on the river, but a canoeist's position can be determined by reference to natural landmarks, such as islands, rapids, and rock formations, or man-made features, such as bridges, towns, or buildings. The mileage indicated on the actual DRBC maps is sometimes inconsistent; for example, the same feature on adjacent DRBC maps might be indicated by different mileposts. Although the maps in this book are adapted from the DRBC maps, every attempt has been made to refer to the same features by the same mileage. The river guide presents the reader with a mile-by-mile description of what will be encountered on the river. The safest way through major rapids, important natural features, man-made structures, historical events, river access points, and other points of interest are discussed. The river guide often refers to "eddies" and "rifts." In the vernacular of old-time river raftsmen, eddies are the slow pools between rifts, or rapids. The raftsmen

had names for the important eddies and rifts, and though no
longer commonly known, these names are used to the extent possible in this book.

The Delaware River is much more than a body of water flowing
from the mountains to the sea: it is the focus of many fascinating
places and events. The features section of each chapter highlights
points of special interest, including major rapids, communities,
historical events, political controversies, engineering feats, recreational and cultural opportunities, and people. The accounts contained in this book are necessarily brief and therefore incomplete,
but they may stimulate readers to make further inquiries.

The accounts of services available and accessible to canoeists
include camping areas, overnight lodging, canoe liveries, restaurants, and sports shops. For the most part, the services listed are
easily accessible by foot from the river. These listings, which are
not meant to be comprehensive, were compiled at the time of the
composition of this book and of course are subject to change.

THE RIVER

The Delaware River begins at Hancock, New York, and flows
330.7 miles to the Atlantic Ocean at the mouth of Delaware Bay.
Tides surge as far upstream as Trenton, 133 miles from the
mouth. The Delaware ranks seventeenth in length among the nation's rivers, draining 13,000 square miles, about one percent of
the continental United States. Along the 197.5 miles above tidewater, the Delaware flows freely, unimpeded by artificial dams.
There are three low wing dams, but these are constructed at natural rapids and do not significantly raise the level of the water behind them.

There are four major tributaries to the Delaware above Trenton: the East and West Branches, the Neversink River, and the Lehigh River. Each is controlled by dams that impound water in great reservoirs for the use of the cities. There are several secondary tributaries—the Lackawaxen, Mongaup, Bushkill, Flatbrook, Paulinskill, Pequest, Musconetcong, Tohicon, and Assunpink—and scores of minor streams contributing to the flow of the Delaware.

The Delaware River typically runs high with snowmelt and April showers in the spring but ebbs with the coming of summer. Less rain, increased evaporation, and reservoir draw-down often combine to produce extremely low flows by August. The Delaware swells somewhat in the autumn, then freezes over solidly by January.

Sometimes floods have been a problem to communities along the Delaware, especially those resulting from the downpour of hurricanes. In 1955 the effects of two hurricanes combined to wash out many Delaware River bridges and to flood cities and villages along the way. Destructive ice flows have occurred as well.

The Delaware River is relatively free of pollution above Trenton, but this has not always been the case. In the early decades of this century, sewage and industrial waste polluted the river to a great extent. Fortunately, the river is no longer used as a sewer.

Today recreation is one of the major attractions of the Delaware. Every year shad and eels migrate in the river, and many other species of game fish can be caught along the entire length of fresh water. Motorboating and waterskiing are popular in some of the ponded areas. Canoeing, however, is the favorite form of recreation on the river. In recent years inner tubes and rubber rafts have joined in. There are more than 20 river outfitters providing over 5,000 river craft along the Delaware. The uppermost 121 miles of the Delaware are now protected by federal law and managed as recreation areas by the National Park Service.

The Delaware in American History

Dutch explorer Henry Hudson "discovered" the Delaware River in 1609 and described it as "one of the finest, best and pleasantest rivers in the world." The river is named for Lord De la Warr, a colonial governor of Virginia who probably never set eyes on the waterway.

The Delaware River has played an important role in American history, beginning with the communities of Indians and followed by the early settlements of Europeans along its shores, Washington's crossing of the Delaware during the Revolutionary War, and the growth of commerce and industrialization. Competition for use of the Delaware and desire for its control have ignited endless controversies. Among these were the Walking Purchase of 1737, the Lackawaxen Crossing in 1829, the Tocks Island Dam in the 1960s and 1970s, and the Point Pleasant diversion of the present day. In 1954 the Supreme Court of the United States was called upon to apportion the water of the Delaware among the states whose boundaries are defined by the river. The Delaware River Basin Commission, made up of the governors of four states and the U.S. Secretary of the Interior, now oversees the use, development, and conservation of the river.

The first boats to ply the Delaware River were canoes. Before any European had settled near or ever seen the river, when the regions of Trenton, Easton, and Port Jervis were nothing but dense forest, the Lenni Lenape in chestnut-log canoes used the Delaware as an avenue of transportation and communication.

In 1764 Daniel Skinner tied a few logs together and floated them from Cochecton to market at Philadelphia; he was among the first to exploit the potential of the Delaware as a river of commerce. Later, "Durham boats"—shallow hulls 40-, 50-, 60-feet long—shuttled merchandise among the growing villages by the Delaware. In these sturdy crafts on Christmas night in 1776, George Washington and his freezing troops embarked to surprise the enemy at Trenton, an act which turned the tide of the Revolution.

As America prospered, so did commerce on the Delaware. The Durham boats were replaced by canal barges toting coal, lumber, and iron in three major canals parallel to the river. Indeed, there are many people today who recall canalboats passing from Easton, through New Hope, Yardley, and Bristol with their loads of coal for the furnaces of Philadelphia. But except for a few museum pieces, canal barges too have disappeared. The Delaware has lost most of its value as an avenue of commerce.

Even as the Delaware's commercial appeal waned, a new phenomenon grew on the river: canoes began to return! At first, only a few hardy souls in wooden boats ventured out for fishing or vacation excursions. In 1892 J. Wallace Hoff and four compatriots dared to paddle all the way from Balls Eddy to Trenton, a 10-day trip. Then, as access and transport became easier, more and more people took to the Delaware for recreation. The advent of mass-produced canoes and livery operations brought an explosion of canoeing on the river; there are now more than 20 canoe liveries strung from Hancock to Trenton, a few of them with more than one thousand boats. On any summer day as many as 10,000 people may be paddling the river, discovering its charm and excitement. In recent years rubber rafts and inner tubes have joined the veritable flotilla.

Rafting on the Delaware

Today rafting on the Delaware evokes the image of a few friends in a navy-surplus inflatable raft, bobbing over rocks and through rapids. But in the last century rafting had an entirely different connotation. Huge log rafts––up to 215 feet long—were floated by the thousands every spring from the uppermost reaches of the Delaware down to Trenton and Philadelphia, their very structures comprised of timber for market.

When the earliest pioneers settled the upper Delaware Valley, their most formidable task was to clear the forest and make way for their little farm plots. Some of the timber was used to build houses, barns, and churches. More was saved for winter's fuel. But still these uses didn't account nearly for the total timber felled. What was to be done with the excess?

The pioneers were nothing if not resourceful. With their immediate needs satisfied, they turned their attention to the booming growth of cities far downstream. In 1764, when Daniel Skinner of Cochecton bound his extra timber together, climbed on top, and floated two hundred miles to Philadelphia, the lumber-rafting industry of the Delaware was born.

Before long, farming had become merely a sideline of the valley people. Real prosperity was dependent on the annual timber sale. A typical farmer would harvest up to one hundred acres

Timber raft bound for market. The Port Jervis–Matamoras Bridge, built in 1904, is in the background. Photo courtesy of Pike County Historical Society.

of woodland in the fall and winter. The logs were sledded and sluiced to piles near the river's edge. In early spring hired hands made a raft by binding the logs with saplings, ropes, and iron spikes. At the first good flood the raft, piled high with lumber, produce, or charcoal, was careening downstream to market.

The magnitude of the industry should not be underestimated. By 1828 at least 1000 rafts a year passed Lackawaxen. Although the industry peaked in the 1850s, as late as 1875, 3,190 rafts were counted. In 1835 there were 208 sawmills in Sullivan County, New York, alone.

A trip down the Delaware by raft must have been an adventure. The rafts were sent during floods because the improved clearance over rocks and obstructions and swift current made the trip much faster. Rafting from Callicoon to Trenton took only three and a half days in good conditions.

The rafts were made first of pine; then, as this resource was depleted, hemlock became the principal product. The logs and lumber were bound together by a transverse birch pole fastened by bent ashwood. In later days horseshoe-shaped iron spikes were used instead of ash. Huge oars were hung at the upstream and downstream ends, perfectly counterweighted for easy handling, to provide steering. In this way the raft could be moved side-to-side as it floated downstream. A typical raft was 120 feet long, 25 feet wide, and drew 2 feet of water.

A raft builder, acting as steersman, would supervise four or six hired hands (often family) on the trip. After making the trip year after year, many steersmen became known to one another. Some achieved the status of local legend. Daniel Skinner, the "Lord Admiral of the Delaware," was in this class, along with Depue Le Bar of Shawnee; Boney Quillan, the "Poet of the Delaware"; and Deacon Mitchell, who raced from Hancock to Trenton in only two days.

The old dam at Lackawaxen, and numerous bridges with their narrow passages between piers, provided treacherous obstacles. But by far Foul Rift was the most feared. Many rafts were "stove-up" as they smashed the rocks in the mile-long rapid. Those individuals that made it through were almost assured of a dowsing as the raft plunged over the final ledges.

Along the way, about a day's journey apart, certain places became popular as stopping points. Hancock, at the confluence of the East and West Branches, was the jumping-off place for rafters. At Big Eddy (Narrowsburg), rafts were sometimes so densely packed that a person could walk from one shore to the other by hopping from raft to raft. Dingmans Ferry was the next logical way station, then Saunts Eddy just above Easton. Upper Black Eddy was most popular of all; it was a favorite carousing spot for raftsmen.

After delivering their rafts and cargo to market at Easton, Trenton, Bristol or Philadelphia, the raftsmen had a long walk home but, with their satchels full of profit, it was a walk they didn't mind.

Wild and Scenic River

By an act of the United States Congress, 75 miles of the Delaware River from Hancock to Port Jervis is a National Scenic and Recreational River. Of course, the upper Delaware has always been scenic and recreational, without the benefit of any act of Congress. But now, the law requires that the river remain in that condition.

Any long-time canoeist or local resident will confirm that use of the upper Delaware has mushroomed in the last decade. The National Park Service (NPS) estimates that a quarter of a million people canoed, kayaked, fished, or camped on the river in 1981.

By 1990, that number is expected to grow to 400,000. Such heavy demand on a 75-mile-long valley with only 7500 permanent residents has placed an extraordinary burden on local services like law enforcement and trash removal.

To ease these pressures, the National Park Service has worked with the fifteen municipalities and five counties through which the river flows in order to draw up a plan for river use management. The result is a unique strategy of cooperation between federal and local authorities.

Unlike most National Parks, the federal government does not own the land within the river corridor (except for the Park headquarters' site on the Pennsylvania side near Narrowsburg, a bookstore in the old Narrowsburg Arlington Hotel, and the Roebling Aqueduct at Lackawaxen—a total of just over three acres). In exchange for this limited federal control of the land, the riverside towns must enforce land use standards to prevent inappropriate use of the valley. In addition, the federal government provides money to the villages for law enforcement and trash removal— problems greatly aggravated by recreational use of the river.

On the river itself the National Park Service is boss. There are 26 full-time and seasonal NPS rangers patrolling the valley in the summer, in cooperation with state and local conservation officers and police. The pale green NPS skiffs are a familiar sight along the way from Hancock to Port Jervis (indeed, to the water gap itself, as the river from Port Jervis to the gap is within the Delaware Water Gap National Recreational Area, also under control of the NPS). The NPS rangers, relieved from much of their traditional shore duties, can concentrate on making recreation on the upper Delaware a safe and educational experience. Before the NPS presence on the river there were typically ten drownings a year (most often at Skinners Falls); in 1982 there was only one.

Recommendations in the regional plan included the following measures:

1. Establishment of a permanent program of reservoir water releases and maintenance of flow
2. Establishment of a scenic roads program in the valley
3. Protection of river islands
4. Establishment of a "recreation-way" linked by a valley excursion train
5. Control of recreation use through licensing of commercial liveries and, possibly, use of a permit system for canoeists
6. Reduction of conflicts between canoeists and fishermen in use of the river
7. Additional NPS acquisition of crucial lands along the river (no more than 1,450 acres)
8. Development of three visitor-orientation centers, featuring interpretation of the historical, cultural, and natural resources of the river and valley.

Whether the plan is ever put to work remains to be seen. Like any plan, this one is dynamic, subject to revision as conditions—and the understanding of these conditions—change.

The National Park Service sponsors numerous activities on the upper Delaware, including interpretive history and nature walks, canoe instruction and tours, and a "Volunteers in Parks" program in which citizens participate in rescue operations, canoe instruction, and information services. For information call 914/252–3947.

Recently the NPS has set up a special phone number (914/252–7100) for river conditions. A taped message reports weather, water temperature, and river level and provides advice for canoeists.

Water Quality

The United States Environmental Protection Agency considers all of the Delaware River from Hancock to Trenton to be suitable for the protection and propagation of fish, shellfish, and wildlife and safe for recreation in and on the water. Indeed, water quality in the 120 miles from Hancock to the water gap is considered excellent, while from the water gap to Trenton the river is rated "good."

The Delaware was not always so clean. A 1799 survey of the river near Philadelphia noted that the Delaware was becoming contaminated by pollution from ships, public sewers, and wharves. Over the years, the situation became worse and worse. By 1940, aircraft pilots approaching Philadelphia were warned not to be alarmed by the stench of the Delaware River, detectable at 5,000 feet. The polluted waters corroded the hulls of ships. Even in the upstream areas, sewage discharges from Port Jervis, Stroudsburg, and Easton and the inflow of industrial wastes virtually killed segments of the Delaware. Raw sewage dumped into the river consumed most of the oxygen dissolved in the water, suffocating fish and other aquatic life. In the worst places, the river actually ran black and emitted the rotten egg smell of hydrogen sulfide, a gas formed when organic material decays in the absence of oxygen.

By the late 1930s the Delaware River states could stand it no longer. A program to stem the pollution was launched the length of the Delaware River. New laws in 1947 and 1972 established standards and required a special permit for any discharge of wastes into the river. Federal funds were granted for the construction of sewage treatment facilities. By the mid-1970s raw sewage was no longer being dumped into the Delaware River; industrial plants no longer discharged noxious wastes into the water. Use of the river as a sewer had come to an end.

Every year the water quality of the Delaware River improves. The migration of shad, which had disappeared in the early part of the century, has returned and grows larger each year. The water of the Delaware River is clean, clear, and refreshing.

This is not to say that there is no pollution at all in the Delaware River. The treated effluent from village and city sewer systems is still discharged. Canoeists may notice these outfalls—usually along the length of a submerged pipe extending from the shore. A prominent example is the discharge from Easton, which is seen as a gray froth about a mile south of the city. This and other discharges, however, are rapidly absorbed and cleansed. Their effect on the river is negligible. Other pollutants enter the river from nonpoint sources, such as fertilizer runoff from fields, bacteria from livestock pens and pasturelands, and oily contaminants from roads and parking lots. Though the Delaware River is clean enough for fishing and swimming, it is nowhere fit to drink.

CANOE SAFETY

Drownings and near drownings are not at all uncommon on the Delaware River. And a drowning is eight times more likely in a canoeing accident than in any other type of boating mishap. In an average year, 10 people lose their lives in capsizes on the Delaware. Most of these tragedies could have been avoided if only the canoeists had taken proper precautions or if they had not overestimated their abilities.

Most of the thousands of canoeists who paddle the Delaware River are novices, and for many, a trip on the Delaware is their very first canoeing experience. Unfortunately, many beginners do not want to admit to themselves or their fellow canoeists that they are incapable of handling a canoe in all situations. Because of their pride, they do foolish things and take unnecessary chances. Novices should take a look at expert canoeists. Experts always wear life jackets in white water, scout their routes before going through rapids, load their canoes properly, and prepare for emergencies should they arise. Most experts have learned the hard way. They know the experience of capsizing and being swept downstream by the overpowering flow of rapids. They know the effects of cold water and cold air. They have had to pull swamped canoes off rocks in a current. Many have had to rescue, or attempt to rescue, novices who did not know these things. The expert canoeist's pride has been washed away by these close calls. He has learned to respect the river, and he is careful. Beginners must be even more careful.

Since drowning is the greatest danger in canoeing, the greatest single protection is a personal flotation device (PFD), known to many as a life jacket. Federal regulations require that every boat, including canoes, have on board a PFD for each occupant. It is not required that the PFD be worn, but that it be available. It may not be necessary for good swimmers to wear a PFD when paddling in the numerous slow-moving eddies of the Delaware. But every canoeist should wear a PFD when approaching a rapid, in a heavy wind, or in an unknown territory.

Even in slow-moving parts of the river, the current, unlike a swimmer, never tires. In a rapid, however, a person pitched into the water has no chance to overcome the current and can only hope to maneuver himself to safety. It is rare when at least one canoe in a party does not capsize in Skinners Falls, Shohola Rift, Wells Falls, or many of the other rapids along the Delaware.

When this happens, the canoeists are often saved only because they were wearing a PFD.

When a canoe does capsize or swamp in white water, its occupants must know what to do. First, they must get themselves upstream of the canoe. A canoe may appear light and maneuverable, but when filled with water, it becomes a one-ton mass capable of pinning and crushing a person against a rock. The capsized canoeist should make sure that his feet are pointed downstream to kick away from any obstructions that might be encountered. Until the shoreline or assistance is within reach, no attempt should be made to stand up in a rapid. A canoeist's feet can easily become wedged in a crevice or between rocks, with the current forcing the person face first into the water.

Because modern canoes don't sink, they provide additional flotation for capsized canoeists. Ten-foot-long ropes, called painters, may be tied to the bow and stern and dragged through the water, to be grabbed in the event of a capsize. There is no rapid in the Delaware River so long that it cannot be ridden out by a canoeist pitched from his canoe. Once in calmer waters, the canoeist can begin to collect himself as well as his canoe, paddles, and remaining equipment and paraphernalia. (Ideally, all loose gear should be securely tied into the canoe from the outset, in anticipation of such mishaps.)

Novices should not attempt to canoe rapids that are beyond their ability. Beginners should avoid canoeing through Skinners Falls and Wells Falls by portaging around these rapids. In addition, the river segments between Narrowsburg and Port Jervis and between the water gap and Martins Creek are not suitable for beginners. No one should canoe after dark.

The second greatest danger to canoeists is hypothermia, or substantially reduced body temperature. Hypothermia, which can be fatal, causes disorientation, lack of coordination, and drowsiness. It is a more serious threat in the spring and fall months when the water and air are cool, but extended exposure in the summer can cause hypothermia. A person capsized into water below 55° Fahrenheit may be in trouble. The body loses heat 40 times faster in water than in air; under such circumstances hypothermia can begin to take effect in a matter of minutes. The best prevention is staying out of cold water. In the spring the Delaware River runs higher as well as colder, and the rapids are more difficult than during the typically moderate summer flows. Under these conditions canoeing the white water stretches should be attempted only by the experienced, who should dress warmly, bring extra dry clothes, travel in groups, and wear life jackets.

Cuts and scrapes are another hazard. A capsize in a rapid often results in assorted abrasions. Even in slow-moving sections of the river, swimmers frequently strike subsurface rocks. Canoeists should wear sneakers or moccasins at all times (preferably an old pair with holes along the bottom so water can run out). Swimming should be attempted only in areas known to be safe and free of hazards.

Sunburn is probably the most frequent injury suffered. Canoeists, especially beginners, often think that a day on the river is a great time to work on their tans and so go home with severe, blistering sunburns. There is no shade on the river, and the sun blazes down all day long. Reflection off the water makes matters worse. On sunny days an aluminum canoe becomes a reflector oven that will slowly bake its unprotected occupants. For protection against sunburn, bring plenty of lotion, especially for the shoulders and thighs. Keep a hat, long sleeve shirt, and long trousers handy.

In addition, there are numerous minor hazards that may be encountered. The river islands team with mosquitoes and yellow jackets. Poison ivy is thick on the islands and along the shore.

Campfires and stoves often cause burns if not tended properly. Some sections of the river are popular with motorboaters; in these areas canoeists should stay near the shoreline. Although awareness and avoidance of these hazards is the best prevention, every party of canoeists should carry at least one well-stocked first aid kit.

A safe canoe trip makes for a good canoe trip. By taking precautions, using common sense, and staying within the limits of one's ability, canoeists on the Delaware River can be assured of a fun-filled and rewarding experience.

Hancock to Long Eddy

The Delaware River begins just below Hancock, New York, at the confluence of the East and West Branches. It is about 16 miles from the beginning of the river to Long Eddy, making this the shortest section to be described in this book. Pennsylvania Route 191 parallels the river closely for the first 8 miles, while New York Route 97 runs nearby for about 2 miles. Otherwise no major roads approach the river, although there are secondary and un-paved roads within a short walk at all times. Except for Hancock there are no major towns and few services. There are two public access areas on the Pennsylvania bank, one each at Mile 323 and Mile 325.

Since this is the uppermost part of the Delaware River, it is the shallowest and narrowest section. There are no major rapids, and only a few riffles rated as Class I. Several low gravel islands pro-vide shifting channels that can be a challenge to navigation.

The river flows through the Appalachian Plateaus geophysical province, which is composed predominantly of level shale and sandstone rock extending in a broad band from northern New York to northern Alabama. The foothills of New York's Catskill Mountains are to the north, and the northern Pocono Mountains of Pennsylvania are to the south. This area was covered by glaciers within the last 20,000 years.

Now the banks of the Delaware and nearby hills are almost en-tirely clothed in mixed secondary hardwood forest. But in the early and mid-nineteenth century, most of the trees were stripped from the hills and floated downstream to the markets in the big cities below.

Many varieties of waterfowl make their home on and near the river, and small game animals abound in the woods nearby. Whitetail deer are frequently found near the water's edge. Otter slides can be seen on the muddy banks. Black bear, although rarely seen, are not uncommon in the forest.

Flow in the East and West Branches is controlled by the Pepacton and Cannonsville reservoirs respectively. Until the mid-1970s there was no effort to control releases from these reservoirs with respect to effects on the mainstream Delaware. As a result, this section of the Delaware River often ran extremely low in the summertime, sometimes so low that canoes had to be dragged over shallow areas. The nearly stagnant water became so warm that trout and other cold-water fish could not survive. The Delaware River Basin Commission now manages reservoir releases so that there is always enough flow for canoes.

Eel traps, or weirs, are encountered in several places between Hancock and Long Eddy. Eels are fish that resemble three-foot snakes. They are catadromous, living in the upper Delaware and migrating every year to spawn in the sea, travelling only at night during the dark of the moon.

Eel weirs are constructed by building two low stone walls, 50 feet or more in length, which meet at the point of a downstream "V." The migrating eels get funneled to the point of the "V," where they are trapped in a grate from which they are simply raked into burlap bags. Not many Americans appreciate the flavor of eels, so most of the harvest is exported to Europe, where eel is considered a delicacy.

In the years when timber rafting was a major industry on the Delaware River, eel weirs were considered an obstruction and were outlawed. Canoeists today must remember that eel weirs are private property and should pass in the channel to the left or right of the weir wings, never over the rock wings or through the chute at the point of the "V."

All of this section of river is designated as a National Scenic River, and recreation on the river is under the jurisdiction of the National Park Service.

RIVER GUIDE

330.7. The Delaware River begins at the confluence of the East and West Branches, which flow from the Catskill Mountains. The community of Hancock, New York, is one mile upstream on the East Branch. Balls Eddy access area is 4.6 miles upstream on the West Branch and is maintained by the Pennsylvania Fish Commission. There is parking, a boat ramp, trash disposal, and sanitary facilities. There are many unimproved access points on both the East and West Branches.

Point Mountain rises between the East and West Branches just above their confluence. The castlelike edifice atop the mountain is an abandoned chapel and mausoleum.

Downstream from the West Branch, on the right, a sand and gravel spit extends about 100 yards. There is a Class I rapid near the spit.

330.0. Upstream end of a low vegetated gravel bar. Channels to the left and right are passable. Sinuous side channels lead through the bar from the left channel. There is a Class I rapid in both left and right channels near the head of the gravel bar.

329.7. Gravel island ends; a second large vegetated gravel bar begins. There is a Class I rapid in the channel between the islands. Right channel is quite shallow.

329.3. Downstream end of gravel bar.

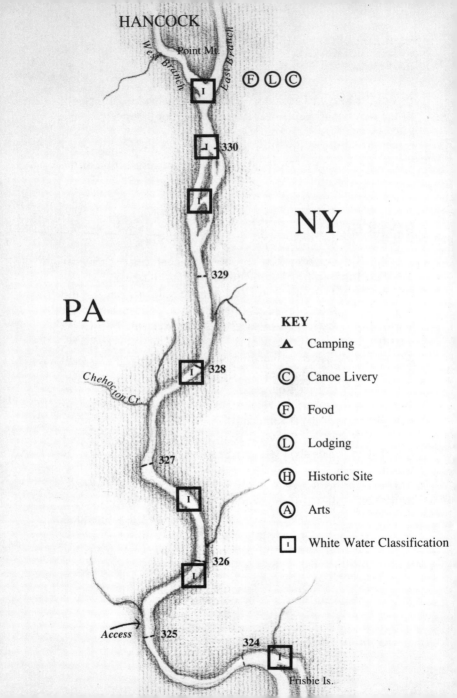

328.0. River bends widely to the right. A rock ledge extending diagonally upstream from the New York bank provides a Class I rapid. Extreme left end of ledge may be hazardous at low water level.

327.2. Chehocton Creek enters, Pennsylvania side.

326.6. Low gravel bar on left. A Class I rapid in the main channel with a few submerged rocks.

325.9. River bends sharply right; very shallow or exposed gravel bar on left. A Class I rapid without obstructions; standing waves to 1½ feet.

325.1. Buckingham access area, Pennsylvania side, maintained by the Pennsylvania Fish Commission. Parking, boat ramp, and trash disposal.

323.7. Upstream end of Frisbie Island, extending .6 mile downstream. Channels to the left and right are passable though shallow. There are Class I rapids without obstruction in the left channel near the upstream end of the island.

323.1. Downstream end of Frisbie Island, with shallows and gravel bars extending a short distance downstream. The channel near the Pennsylvania bank and channels between the gravel bars present Class I rapids.

323.0. Equinunk access area, Pennsylvania side, operated by the Pennsylvania Fish Commission. This is an unimproved gravel access with no facilities.

322.6. Equinunk Creek enters, Pennsylvania side, with gravel bars extending into the river. The community of Equinunk, Pennsylvania, is on the right.

321.7. A Class I rapid without obstructions.

321.6. Abutments of the old Lordville Bridge, constructed in 1903, demolished by the New York Dept. of Transportation in 1987 for safety reasons. The community of Lordville, New York, is on the right.

321.0. A small stream enters, New York side. Just below the

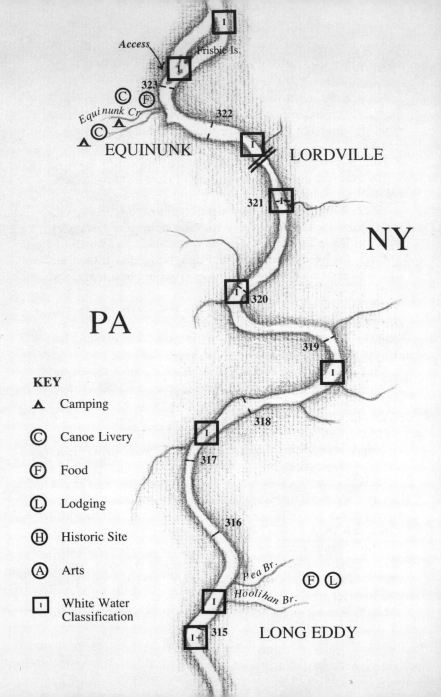

KEY

▲ Camping

© Canoe Livery

Ⓕ Food

Ⓛ Lodging

Ⓗ Historic Site

Ⓐ Arts

☐ White Water
  Classification

Access

Frisbie Is.

323

Equi nunk Cr.

EQUINUNK

322

LORDVILLE

321

NY

PA

320

319

318

317

316

Pea Br.

Hoolihan Br.

Ⓕ Ⓛ

315

LONG EDDY

stream is a Class I rapid with submerged and protruding boulders on the left.

320.1. Shallows or exposed gravel bars on the right. A Class I rapid without obstructions.

319.7. River bends sharply left.

318.8. River bends sharply right. Right side is quite shallow. There is a Class I rapid along the left bank for .3 mile.

317.6. River broadens and becomes very shallow. Gravel may be exposed on the right and left center.

317.2. River continues very shallow on right; exposed gravel bars at low water level. River bends widely left. A Class I rapid around exposed or submerged boulders in the middle of the channel.

315.7. Pea Brook enters, New York side. River narrows to the right.

315.6. Hoolihan Brook enters, New York side, with gravel deposits extending into the river. The community of Long Eddy, New York, is on the left. Enter a Class I rapid with no obstructions.

CAMPING AND SERVICES

Camping

Although here the river is designated as a National Wild and Scenic River and is under the jurisdiction of the National Park Service, the Park Service maintains no public campgrounds. Virtually all of the land adjacent to the river is private, and camping is restricted to established campgrounds. Canoeists who camp on the riverbanks without permission are trespassers, and many have been arrested in recent years. There are two private campgrounds located in this section of the river:

1. Riverside Campground (P.O. Box 36, Equinunk, Pennsylvania 18417, 717/224–6410).
2. River Valley Campground (R.D. 1, Box 8A, Equinunk, Pennsylvania 18417, 717/224–4083).

Canoe Liveries

1. Bob and Rick Landers' Delaware River Canoe Trips (Box 376, Narrowsburg, New York 12764, 914/252–3925) began in 1955. One of the giant Delaware River outfitters, Landers operates a canoe base on the East Branch about 2 miles upstream from the confluence of the West Branch, with access from New York Route 17. Portage is available.
2. Delaware Excursions, Inc. (Warners Wood, Box 110A, Equinunk, Pennsylvania 18417, 717/224–4648) rents canoes with access from Pennsylvania Route 191.
3. River Valley Campgrounds (R.D. 1, Box 8A, Equinunk, Pennsylvania 18417, 717/224–4083) rents canoes from its Equinunk campground near Pennsylvania Route 191.

Other Services

All services accessible in this section of the river are clustered in the riverside hamlets.

330.7 Hancock, New York. Located between the East and West Branches of the Delaware about one mile upstream from their confluence. Two supermarkets and several restaurants, in-

Opposite: Confluence of the East and West Branches. The Delaware River begins here, just south of Hancock, New York. Point Mountain rises between the branches. Photo courtesy of James M. Staples.

cluding the Stage Door, Star Restaurant, Delaware Inn, Candyland, and the Pickle Barrel Deli.

322.5 Equinunk, Pennsylvania:

1. Equinunk Inn, a tavern with sandwiches available.
2. Hunt's Country Store, provisions and merchandise.
3. Village Barn Restaurant, with table and counter service.

315.4 Long Eddy, New York. Unimproved access from the river just downstream from Hoolihan Brook, then .2 mile up the road to Long Eddy.

1. Bruno's General Store, merchandise and provisions.
2. Long Eddy Hotel, open to guests in the summer.
3. Ginger's Country Store (on New York 97, .2 mile from the intersection), luncheonette, pizza, provisions.
4. Wanda's Luncheonette (.25 mile south of the intersection on New York 97), fried food, sandwiches, soda.

Long Eddy to Narrowsburg

It is about 26 miles between Long Eddy and Narrowsburg. With the inflow of numerous small streams, the flow of the Delaware is slightly greater than in the preceding river section, although for the most part it remains shallow and narrow. There are interesting Class I to II rapids just below Long Eddy and Hankins, as well as famous Skinners Falls, a severe Class II rapid at Mile 295.2. There are numerous low gravel islands, many of which are submerged at higher water level.

Callicoon and Narrowsburg, New York, are the principal towns in this section, although services can also be found in several places along New York Route 97, which is close to the river most of the way. Secondary roads approach the river on the Pennsylvania side at Callicoon and between Damascus and Narrowsburg. The Erie Railroad continues to run very close to the river on the New York bank. There are seven public access areas, two each at Callicoon (Mile 303.5), Cochecton (Mile 298.4), and Narrowsburg and one at the Milanville Bridge just above Skinners Falls.

The river continues to flow through the Appalachian Plateaus geophysical province. There are several locations of exposed bedrock, the most prominent at Skinners Falls. The banks of the river are almost entirely forested, although in a few areas fields have been cleared for farming. Water birds are especially abundant here. About 20 American bald eagles make their winter home in the nearby hills, but few eagles are sighted in the summer.

The river here is designated as a National Scenic and Recreational River, and recreation on the river is under the jurisdiction of the National Park Service.

RIVER GUIDE

315.7. Pea Brook enters, New York side. River narrows considerably to the right as gravel deposits encroach on the left.

315.6. Hoolihan Brook enters, New York side. Gravel bar at mouth of stream extends into the river. The community of Long Eddy, New York, is on the left. Enter a Class I rapid; no obstructions.

315.0. A low vegetated gravel bar on the left. The left channel is very shallow at low water. There is a Class I + rapid between the Pennsylvania shore and the gravel bar.

314.9. Downstream end of gravel bar. Shallows or exposed gravel in the right channel; standing waves to 1½ feet on the right.

314.1. Basket Creek enters, New York side. Extensive gravel bar at mouth of creek extends to middle of river and downstream. New York Route 97 crosses Basket Creek on a high concrete bridge.

314.0. Class I rapid with no obstructions.

313.4. Class I rapid with no obstructions.

312.7. Little Equinunk Creek enters, Pennsylvania side. There is a Class I rapid between the gravel bars at the mouth of the creek and the New York bank.

312.6. Pass under the Kellams-Stalker Bridge. Completed in 1890, this is the third-oldest existing span across the Delaware. The suspension cables hang below the one-lane road surface in the center.

311.5. A small creek enters from a marshy area on the Pennsyl-

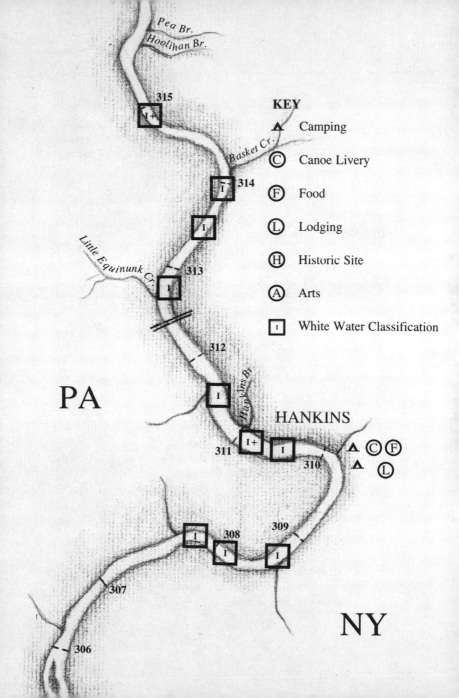

Pea Br.

Hoolihan Br.

315

KEY

▲ Camping

Ⓒ Canoe Livery

Ⓕ Food

Ⓛ Lodging

Ⓗ Historic Site

Ⓐ Arts

☐ White Water Classification

Basket Cr.

I+

I 314

I

313

Little Equinunk Cr.

I

312

PA

I

Hankins Br.

HANKINS

I+ I

311 310

▲ Ⓒ Ⓕ

▲ Ⓛ

309

I 308

I

I

307

NY

306

vania side. A Class I rapid continues for .2 mile. A few submerged and protruding boulders in left center may be a hazard.

310.9. Hankins Brook enters, New York side. Gravel deposits from the creek narrow the river considerably, creating a Class I + rapid with standing waves to 1½ feet.

310.8. Class I rapid continues over submerged boulders. Very shallow on the left. The community of Hankins, New York, is on the left.

310.0. River bends sharply to the right.

308.5. River continues right turn. A Class I rapid, with boulders and submerged ledges near the New York side.

308.1. A Class I rapid extending .3 mile; no obstructions.

307.9. River is pooled for next 2 miles.

305.8. Upstream end of large vegetated gravel island. Right channel is passable, but boulders protrude at low water. Main current flows through left channel. There are large boulders near the left bank.

305.5. Downstream end of gravel bar. A Class I rapid in the left channel without obstructions. There is a small gravel bar in the middle of the channel at the downstream end of the island.

305.1. Hollister Creek enters, Pennsylvania side. A gravel bar at the mouth of the creek extends halfway across the river. There is a Class I rapid between the bar and the New York bank. Submerged boulders on left may be hazardous.

304.4. Upstream end of a low vegetated gravel island. The island is submerged at moderately high water level.

There is an active eel weir in the left channel at the head of the island. The left channel is passable to the right of the eel weir, but shallow.

The right channel, though narrower, is deeper. A small gravel island in the right channel begins just below the head of the main island. The main channel is left of the smaller island.

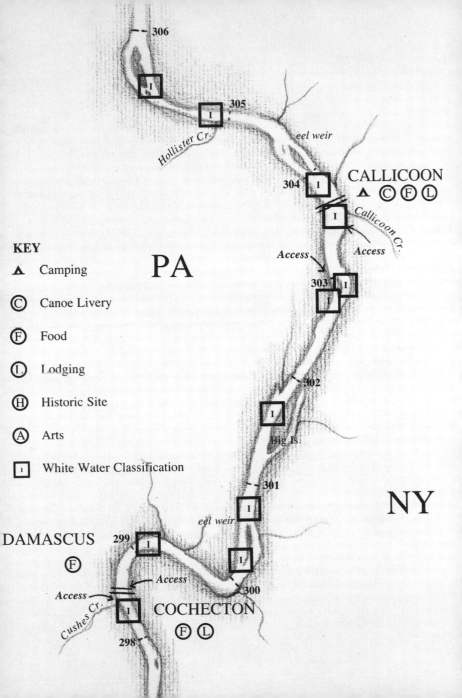

304.0. Gravel bar ends. Another gravel island begins. There is a Class I rapid over the shallows between the islands and along the Pennsylvania shore.

303.7. Pass under the modern concrete Callicoon Bridge, constructed in 1961. A short Class I rapid immediately past bridge. The community of Callicoon, New York, is on the left. Callicoon Creek enters, New York side. A wide gravel bar at the mouth of the creek extends halfway across the river.

303.6. Callicoon access area, New York side. Maintained by the New York Department of Environmental Conservation, this location provides ample parking, a boat launch, trash disposal, and sanitary facilities. The National Park Service maintains an information booth here.

303.1. Callicoon access area, Pennsylvania side, maintained by the Pennsylvania Fish Commission. There is a boat ramp, trash disposal, sanitary facilities, and ample parking.

303.0. Upstream end of a low gravel island; submerged at moderately high water. Channels left and right of the island are passable with Class I rapids.

302.9. Downstream end of gravel island. Another small gravel bar and shallows in the middle of the river.

301.9. A small creek enters from behind a gravel spit, Pennsylvania side. A Class I rapid with no obstructions.

301.2. Downstream end of Big Island, a large vegetated gravel bar on the left. The left channel is dry at the upstream end of the "island."

300.5. A Class I rapid over shallows; no obstructions.

300.3. Upstream end of a low vegetated gravel island; mostly submerged at moderately high water. The left channel is very shallow and may be blocked by gravel bars at very low water. There is an active eel weir in the right channel at the head of the island. Canoes can pass between the island and the left wing of the eel weir.

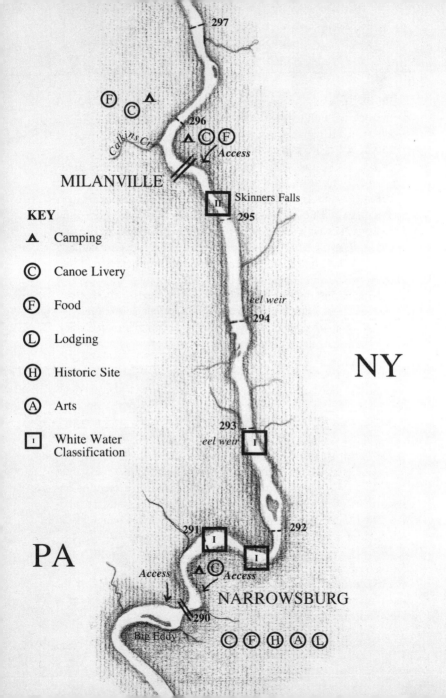

297

F ▲
C
Calkins Cr.

296

▲ C F
← *Access*

MILANVILLE

▉ Skinners Falls
295

KEY

▲ Camping

C Canoe Livery

F Food

L Lodging

H Historic Site

A Arts

▉ White Water
Classification

eel weir
294

NY

293
eel weir ▉

291
▉
292
▉

PA

Access
▲ C *Access*
↓

NARROWSBURG
290

Big Eddy

C F H A L

300.0. Tapered downstream end of gravel island. Class I rapid over shallows without obstructions.

299.9. River bends sharply to the right.

299.1. A Class I rapid without obstructions.

298.5. Cochecton access area, New York side. Limited parking, sanitary facilities, and trash disposal.

298.4. Pass under the steel-truss Cochecton-Damascus Bridge, built in 1952. The communities of Cochecton, New York, and Damascus, Pennsylvania, are at opposite ends of the bridge.

298.3. Damascus access area, Pennsylvania side, maintained by the Pennsylvania Fish Commission, which provides parking, trash disposal, and sanitary facilities. The National Park Service maintains an information kiosk here.

Cushes Creek enters, Pennsylvania side, at the access area.

297.8. A low vegetated gravel bar in the middle of the river; submerged at moderately high water. Left channel is narrow and shallow but passable.

296.5. A low vegetated gravel bar on left. Channel left of the bar may be too shallow for passage at low water. River bends to the right.

295.6. Calkins Creek enters, Pennsylvania side.

295.4. Pass under the Milanville – Skinners Falls Bridge. Built in 1901, this steel-truss span has a wood-plank road surface. Milanville, Pennsylvania, is on the right. Skinners Falls access area, New York side, maintained by the New York Department of Environmental Conservation, provides ample parking, sanitary facilities, and trash disposal. The National Park Service maintains an information kiosk here.

295.3. Large angular boulders on the left signal the approach to Skinners Falls.

295.2. Enter Skinners Falls, a Class II rapid and one of the most severe rifts on the Delaware River. (See the description in the features section of this chapter.)

Skinners Falls, River Mile 295.2. One of the most hazardous rapids on the Delaware. Nearly horizontal slabs of sandy shale provide a challenging series of ledges. Photo by the author.

295.1. Skinners Falls ends. River is ponded for next 2 miles.

294.1. An active eel weir, left center of river. Passage is clear near New York bank and right side of river.

293.7. River narrows with a broad sand and gravel bar on the right. There are two low gravel bars in the main channel, submerged at moderately high water. An abandoned eel weir, left side of river, can be passed over at moderate water level. Rocks on the left may be a hazard.

293.0. An active eel weir, middle of the river. Passage around the weir on the left and right presents Class I rapids.

292.1. A large low vegetated gravel bar, middle of the river. Passage is clear in left and right channels.

291.6. River bends sharply right.

291.3. A Class I rapid over ledges extending across the river. Main channel is in right center with standing waves to 1½ feet.

291.0. Class I rapid continues over ledges.

290.9. An unnamed stream enters, Pennsylvania side, with extensive marshy areas on the right.

290.5. River bends sharply left and becomes quite narrow.

290.1. Narrowsburg access area, New York side. Ample parking, paved boat ramp, trash disposal, and sanitary facilities. Maintained by the New York Department of Environmental Conservation. The National Park Service maintains an information booth here.

290.0. Pass under the arched Narrowsburg Bridge, constructed in 1954 to replace an old covered bridge. Rock ledges are on the left. The community of Narrowsburg, New York, stands at the left end of the bridge. (See the features section of this chapter.)

FEATURES

Skinners Falls

The sign hanging from the Milanville Bridge warns, "Danger—rapids ahead. Seven persons drown here in an average year." From the bridge the ominous rumble of Skinners Falls can be heard, and a spray of white water can be seen leaping from the river surface downstream. Skinners Falls is the first major rapid on the Delaware River, considered by many the most hazardous.

The popularity of Skinners Falls is a major reason for the high number of drownings. Since the National Park Service began patrolling the area, casualties have tapered off, but Skinners Falls nevertheless remains a treacherous rift. Near disasters occur regu-

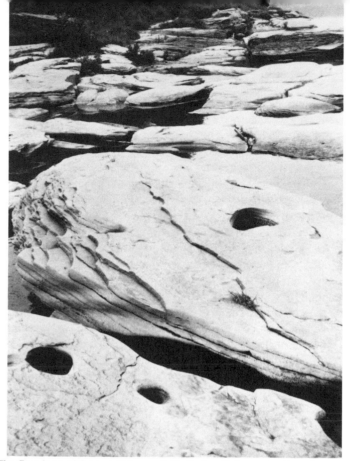

The flow is so violent at Skinners Falls that potholes up to three feet deep have been worn in the exposed bedrock. Photo by the author.

larly every summer. One typical day in 1976 a group of 16 canoeists from the Staten Island Italian–American Club, on their first canoe trip, approached Skinners Falls. The men wore no life jackets and made no effort to reconnoiter their route through the rift. The first of the eight canoes bobbed through without incident, but the second capsized in the high standing waves and pitched its occupants and all their gear into the rushing water. The third canoe caught on a rock, turned sideways, and rolled into a hydraulic below one of the ledges. The remaining five canoes likewise capsized or swamped. Several of the canoeists were poor swimmers and were rescued luckily by other boaters. Two of the swamped canoes drifted on downstream while their occupants swam to the safety of shore. Every person in the group no doubt went home somewhat wiser in the ways of the river.

Skinners Falls, also known as Cochecton Falls, is named for Daniel Skinner, the first individual, tradition has it, to float timber rafts from the upper Delaware to market at Philadelphia. The Skinner family had extensive land holdings in the area around the falls.

A pass through Skinners Falls requires every safety precaution. Life jackets must be worn securely. Heavily loaded canoes should be emptied of their gear, which can be portaged over trails along either side of the river. Canoeists should stop and carefully reconnoiter their route between the boulders, ledges, and standing waves. When Hoff's party explored the Delaware in 1892, they elected to portage around Skinners Falls entirely. This is a wise choice for any novice.

The approach to Skinners Falls begins with large squarish boulders on the left side of the river. The actual falls consists of four increasingly severe ledges extending across the river. Nearly horizontal slabs of shale are exposed at the New York bank, plunging gently toward Pennsylvania and forming the ledges making Skinners Falls. The best specific route through the falls varies dramatically with the water level, though the main passage is in the right center. Even there high standing waves and submerged boulders can capsize the most experienced canoeists. The final ledge creates a potentially dangerous hydraulic in the middle and left of the river and must be carefully avoided.

The water flows so violently at Skinners Falls that three-feet-deep potholes have been gouged in the bedrock. Several are clearly visible in the exposed ledges on the left.

There is a major public access area and Bob Landers' Campground on the New York bank just upstream from Skinners Falls. The National Park Service maintains an information booth here, and frequently rangers are present to assist canoeists. There are wide trails on both sides of the river along Skinners Falls. Novices can portage their gear and canoes along these trails, while more proficient canoeists can use the trails to take their canoes back upstream for one more run.

Narrowsburg

This little village on the banks of the Delaware has not changed much in the last century. Originally known as Big Eddy, it was once an important stopping place for timber raftsmen. The New York and Erie Railroad, built through Narrowsburg in 1849, brought permanent settlers and a well-defined business district. The centerpiece of Narrowsburg was, and still is, the Arlington Hotel, three stories high with broad planked balconies. On his 1892 Delaware canoe adventure J. Wallace Hoff stayed at the Arlington and remarked on the hospitality and attractive waitresses. Today the Arlington is listed on the National Historic Register and is occupied by the Delaware Valley Arts Alliance. The National Park Service operates an information center and bookstore on the ground floor.

Half a mile from the Delaware River bridge at Narrowsburg stands Fort Delaware, a museum of colonial history. The Sullivan County Department of Public Works maintains the fort, which has been constructed according to the specifications of the pioneer settlement at nearby Cushetunk. Fort Delaware, with its log

Narrowsburg, New York. The river is 113 feet deep just downstream from the bridge—the deepest point on the Delaware. Photo courtesy of James M. Staples.

stockades and guardposts, is open to the public in the summer for a nominal fee. Costumed guides demonstrate what life on the eighteenth-century Delaware River frontier might have been like.

Narrowsburg is crowded against the Delaware River, and all services are within easy walking distance. Located on Main Street (parallel to the river) are Keenan's Pharmacy, Narrowsburg Bakery (Saturday and Sunday only), Midtown Cafe (with table and counter service), and Ken's Sport Shop. Stranahan's Hardware, on Main Street near the Old Arlington Hotel, has groceries and general merchandise.

Kelly's Oasis, an ice cream parlor and restaurant, is located on Pennsylvania Route 652, .1 mile from the river. Robbie's Restaurant is .1 mile further on New York Route 97, very near Bob Landers' Campground and Canoe Base.

CAMPING AND SERVICES

Camping

This entire section of the Delaware River is under the jurisdiction of the National Park Service, but lands adjacent to the river are mostly privately owned. Camping is restricted to established campgrounds unless permission is first obtained from the landowner.

1. Red Barn Family Campground (Hankins, New York 12741, 914/887–4995) is located on the river at Mile 310.9.
2. The Hankins House (Route 97, Hankins, New York 12741, 914/887–4423) has sites for campers as well as hotel rooms. Located on Route 97 about .1 mile from the river at Mile 310.9.
3. Upper Delaware Campgrounds (Box 331, Callicoon, New York 12723, 914/887–5344/5110) is a full service campground on the river's edge just downstream from Callicoon Creek. There are more than 225 sites, modern sanitary facilities with showers, a swimming pool, ice, firewood, and a camp store.
4. Bob and Rick Landers' Delaware River Canoe Trips (Box

376, Narrowsburg, New York 12764, 914/252–3925)
maintains a large campground in a field at the New York
end of the Milanville–Skinners Falls Bridge. There are tent
sites and lean-tos, sanitary facilities with showers, water,
ice, firewood, and supplies.

5. Cushetunk Campground (Box 3, Milanville, Pennsylvania
   18443, 717/729–7984) is near the Pennsylvania end of the
   Milanville–Skinners Falls Bridge.

6. Bob and Rick Landers' Delaware River Canoe Trips (see
   above) has another large campground on the bluffs over-
   looking the river just upstream from the Narrowsburg
   Bridge. Tent sites, lean-tos, sanitary facilities with showers, ice, supplies, and firewood are available. The community of Narrowsburg is accessible from this site.

Canoe Liveries

1. Bob and Rick Landers' Delaware River Canoe Trips (Box
   376, Narrowsburg, New York 12764, 914/252–3925) operates four bases in this section. With over 1300 canoes, it is
   one of the giants among Delaware River outfitters. Portage
   is available to most upper Delaware access points. Bob Landers' also rents kayaks, rafts, and inner tubes. An annual
   "Dash and Splash" race, on foot to Skinners Falls and by canoe back to Narrowsburg, is held here in early May.

   a. Hankins Canoe Base, access from New York Route
      97.

   b. Callicoon Canoe Base, access from Main Street
      near the Callicoon Bridge, with canoe launch into
      Callicoon Creek which soon joins the Delaware.

   c. Skinners Falls Canoe Base, associated with Landers'
      Campground at the New York end of the Milanville
      –Skinners Falls Bridge.

d. Narrowsburg Canoe Base, at Landers' Narrowsburg Campground, access from New York Route
97, .4 mile north of the Narrowsburg Bridge.

2. Hankins House (Route 97, Hankins, New York 12741,
914/887–4423) rents canoes from its hotel and restaurant
on Route 97 in Hankins.

3. Outdoor Adventure, Ltd. (Box 331, Callicoon, New York
12723, 914/887–5344/5110), associated with Upper Delaware Campgrounds, has over 300 Coleman and Grumman
canoes available for rent at Upper Delaware Campgrounds,
near the south end of Main Street, Callicoon, New York.

4. Kittatinny Canoes (Dingmans Ferry, Pennsylvania 18328,
717/828–2700/2338), the oldest and one of the largest Delaware River canoe outfitters, operates its northernmost canoe base on the Pennsylvania shore near the Milanville–
Skinners Falls Bridge. Livery service is available from
any of Kittatinny's downstream bases.

5. Cushetunk Canoe Rentals (Box 3, Milanville, Pennsylvania
18443, 717/729–7984) has canoes available for rent at its
campground on the Delaware at Milanville.

6. J&J Canoe Rentals (P.O. Box 136, Narrowsburg, New
York 12764, 914/252–6824) operates its main base in
Narrowsburg.

Other Services

All services accessible in this section are clustered in the riverside hamlets.

310.2 Hankins, New York:

1. Bennett's General Store, with sandwiches, cold cuts, general merchandise.

2. Hankins House, lodging, restaurant, and tavern.

303.7 Callicoon, New York. Many services available, including supermarket, produce, variety store, laundromat, and pharmacy.

1. Western Hotel, cafe and tavern with a few rooms available.
2. Century Hotel, restaurant and lodging.
3. Wagon Wheel Restaurant, breakfast, lunch, and dinner.
4. Autumn Inn, restaurant, breakfast, lunch, and dinner.
5. Robby's Restaurant.
6. Rod's Taxidermy and Sport Shop.

298.4 Cochecton New York:

1. Cochecton General Store and Deli, .2 mile north of Cochecton-Damascus Bridge.
2. My Place Motel, between the river and railroad, .2 mile from the general store.

298.4 Damascus, Pennsylvania. A summer snack trailer frequently parks at the Damascus access area just downstream from the Cochecton-Damascus Bridge.

295.4 Skinners Falls, New York. Bob Landers operates a general store in association with its campground and canoe base at the New York end of the Milanville–Skinners Falls Bridge.

295.4 Milanville, Pennsylvania. The Milanville General Store and Deli, with sandwiches, soda, and general merchandise, is .3 mile from the Milanville–Skinners Falls Bridge in Pennsylvania.

290.0 Narrowsburg, New York, is described in detail in the features section of this chapter.

Narrowsburg to Barryville

Most of this section of the river passes through an undeveloped near wilderness. No principal road approaches the river for the first 10 miles, though between Minisink Ford and Barryville, New York, Route 97 closely parallels the river on the left. The Erie Railroad is atop the New York bank for the first 5 miles, then crosses to follow the river on the Pennsylvania side for the remaining distance. Narrowsburg is the only town, but some services can be found at the crossroads communities of Lackawaxen, Minisink Ford, Barryville, and Shohola. The total distance between Narrowsburg and Barryville is 16.5 miles.

This section of the Delaware is dramatically different from the preceding ones. Below the Big Eddy pool at Narrowsburg, the deepest water on the Delaware between its source and the mouth of Delaware Bay, the river falls over a series of exposed bedrock ledges, creating exciting rapids. Ten-Mile Rift, West Colang Rift, Narrows Falls Rift, and Big Cedar Rift are rated as Class II rapids, while there are 24 rapids less than Class II. This part of the Delaware River is not suitable for beginners.

The river continues through the Appalachian Plateaus geophysical province; outcrops of characteristic shale and sandstone rock occur frequently. The banks are wooded almost entirely in mixed deciduous forests; however, some areas have been cleared for farming or recreational use. This section of the Delaware is the main spawning area for the American shad, an anadromous fish living most of its life in the ocean, but migrating into fresh water to spawn. Shad begin their annual run up the Delaware in late spring and arrive here by mid-summer. In the early decades of the twentieth century, the shad migration was almost wiped out by pollution, but in recent years it has made a strong comeback.

The Delaware and Hudson Canal once paralleled the river on the New York bank below Lackawaxen. Now only its traces remain. The canal was carried across the river on the suspension bridge at Lackawaxen. Lackawaxen was also the home of cowboy author Zane Grey and the site of the bloody Revolutionary battle of Minisink.

This section is designated as a National Wild and Scenic River, and recreation on the river is under the jurisdiction of the National Park Service. There are three public access areas, two at Narrowsburg and the other at Lackawaxen. Many private outfitters maintain canoe bases along New York Route 97 between Minisink Ford and Barryville.

RIVER GUIDE

290.0. Pass under the arched span of Narrowsburg Bridge. The community of Narrowsburg, New York, is on the left. Enter Big Eddy, the deepest pool in the Delaware River, where the river bottom is 113 feet below the surface. The current at the surface of Big Eddy flows in a circle and is in an upstream direction on the left. Big Eddy was a favorite stopping place for timber raftsmen in the nineteenth century.

289.9. Narrowsburg access area, Pennsylvania side, maintained by the Pennsylvania Fish Commission. Parking, paved boat ramp, and trash disposal.

289.1. River becomes shallow and bends sharply left.

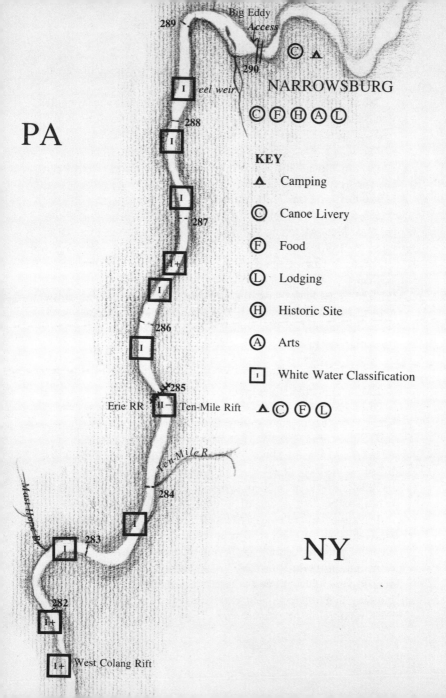

289

Big Eddy
Access

290

Ⓒ ▲

NARROWSBURG

Ⓒ Ⓕ Ⓗ Ⓐ Ⓛ

PA

I *eel weir*

288

I

I

287

I +

I

286

I

×285

Erie RR II− Ten-Mile Rift

Ten-Mile R.

284

I

Mast Hope R.

I 283

282

I+

I+ West Colang Rift

NY

KEY

▲ Camping

Ⓒ Canoe Livery

Ⓕ Food

Ⓛ Lodging

Ⓗ Historic Site

Ⓐ Arts

I White Water Classification

▲ Ⓒ Ⓕ Ⓛ

288.3. An active eel weir in left center. In the passage along the Pennsylvania shore there is a Class I rapid with no obstructions.

287.7. Class I rapid; no obstructions.

287.2. A Class I rapid. Rock ledges extend from Pennsylvania shore; gravel bars and shallows on left. Main channel with standing waves to 1½ feet is in left center.

286.8. Numerous boulders protrude from water.

286.6. Class I + rapid in a river narrows. Bouders on right may be hazardous. Main channel is left center. Diminishes to a class I rapid in .2 mile.

285.6. A Class I rapid with a few submerged and protruding boulders.

285.0. Pass under three-truss span of Erie Railroad Bridge. Enter Ten-Mile Rift, a Class II − rapid. Current quickens as it passes under the bridge. Beware of bridge piers. Rift is short, with its main channel in right center.

Ten-Mile River Boy Scout Camp, a 14,000-acre reservation, is on the New York shore.

284.0. Ten-Mile River enters, New York side.

283.6. A boulder ledge across the river presents a Class I rapid. There is a clear channel in left center with standing waves to 1½ feet. Submerged rocks on right may be a hazard.

282.7. A Class I rapid. Watch for submerged and protruding boulders.

282.4. Mast Hope Brook enters, Pennsylvania side. River bends sharply left.

The little village of Mast Hope is on the Pennsylvania bank. According to tradition this location was the "last hope" for discovering a tree tall enough to become the main mast of the U.S.S. Constitution, "Old Ironsides." Although much of the timber cut here in the eighteenth and nineteenth centuries was used in ship-building at Philadelphia, it is unlikely that the 104-foot mast of the Constitution originated here. The historic Mast Hope plank house is about 100 yards up the road from the river.

282.0. A Class I+ rapid, beginning with moderate riffles over boulder ledges, then becoming more severe as the river bends slightly right. Considerable maneuvering is required to avoid submerged boulders. The channel on the left is clear but shallow.

281.4. Enter West Colang Rift, beginning as a Class I+ rapid, extending .3 mile. The rapid begins in a shallows peppered with numerous submerged boulders. The clearest channel is on the right. The red-roofed bungalows of Camp Colang, a private camp, are on the Pennsylvania shore.

281.1. West Colang Rift becomes a Class II rapid in its final drop. Boulders on the left are a serious hazard. The main channel is in river center, but maneuvering is necessary to avoid rocks.

281.0. Camp Colang's boat dock, Pennsylvania shore.

280.5. West Colang Creek enters, Pennsylvania side.

280.3. River bends sharply left.

280.1. A Class I rapid. River is very shallow at low water level.

279.4. Enter Narrows Falls Rift, a Class II— rapid. At moderate and low water level, considerable maneuvering is required to avoid submerged and protruding rocks. The left side is too shallow for passage. The main channel flows in right center, with standing waves to 2 feet, but boulders repeatedly redirect the flow. Capsizing is very common in this rift.

279.0. New York Route 97 approaches closely on the left, the first major road to do so since Narrowsburg.

278.7. A Class I rapid without significant hazards.

278.3. York Lake Creek enters, New York side.

277.7. The Lackawaxen River enters, Pennsylvania side. At moderately high water level, the Lackawaxen River presents Class II, III and IV rapids in its course from Honesdale, Pennsylvania.

277.6. The Lackawaxen access area, Pennsylvania side, main-

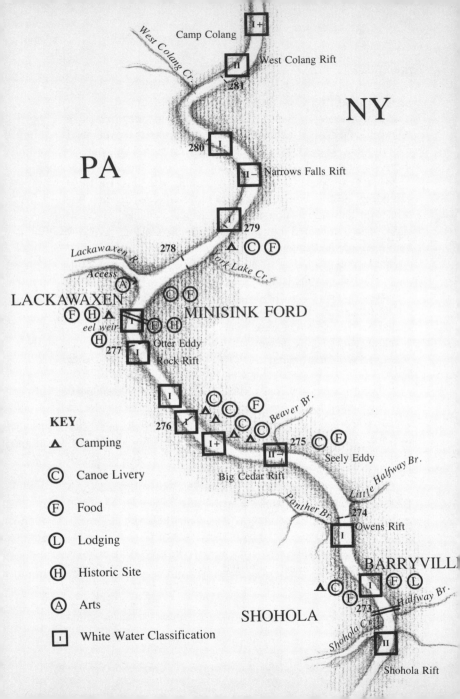

tained by the Pennsylvania Fish Commission. Paved boat ramp, ample parking, and trash disposal. The National Park Service maintains an information booth here. The Zane Grey Inn and Museum, home of author Zane Grey, stands opposite the access area. (See the features section of this chapter.)

277.4. Pass under the Lackawaxen pedestrian bridge, built in 1848 by John Roebling to carry the D&H canal. This bridge is a National Historic Landmark. (See the features section of this chapter.)

There is a wide gravel bar on the left just past the bridge.

277.3. An active eel weir in the middle of the river. There is a Class I rapid over the shallows right of the weir.

Enter Otter Eddy; slow water for .6 mile.

276.7. Rock Rift, a Class I rapid without obstructions.

Eel weir. Constructed of 50-foot-long stone wings to funnel eels into a grate at the apex. Eel weirs are private property, and canoeists must be careful to paddle around the wings. Photo by the author.

276.3. A Class I rapid with a few submerged and protruding boulders on the right.

275.9. Another Class I rapid. Boulders protrude on right.

275.6. A Class I + rapid. A rock ledge extends diagonally upstream from the New York side. The main channel, with standing waves to 1½ feet, is in the right center.

275.0. Beaver Brook enters, New York side. Enter Big Cedar Rift, beginning as a Class I rapid then building to a Class II −. The river falls over two boulder ledges with the best passage in the middle, then opens into an area of scattered submerged and protruding boulders.

274.9. The final ledge of Big Cedar Rift, with a clear channel in the middle. At low water the ledge cannot be penetrated on the right. Haystack waves to 2 feet. Enter Seely Eddy, extending one mile.

274.0. Little Halfway Brook enters, New York side.

273.9. Panther Brook enters, Pennsylvania side.

273.8. Enter Owens Rift, a Class I rapid, very shallow at low water level.

273.3. A Class I rapid without obstructions. The abutments of the old Shohola Bridge, built originally in 1855 and closed in 1941, are visible on the Pennsylvania bank.

273.0. Pass under the three-truss span of the Shohola-Barryville Bridge, constructed in 1941.

FEATURES

Roebling Bridge, Lackawaxen

The old bridge at Lackawaxen is one of six suspension bridges spanning the canoeable portion of the Delaware River. (A suspension bridge is constructed by hanging the roadway from cables suspended across the river.) Downstream from Trenton, the Ben Franklin and Walt Whitman bridges at Philadelphia and the double-spanned Delaware Memorial Bridge are built upon the same principle. Across the country most of the great bridges —the Brooklyn, George Washington, Verrazano Narrows, and Golden Gate—are suspension bridges. But the little bridge at Lackawaxen is special. It is the oldest suspension bridge in America, built by John Roebling, a pioneer of modern civil engineering most famous for his design of the Brooklyn Bridge.

The great stone piers and heavy steel cables of the Lackawaxen bridge seem unnecessarily massive for the narrow pedestrian walkway. The apparent strength of its construction, however, is a clue to this bridge's history. The Delaware and Hudson Canal, between Honesdale, Pennsylvania, and Rondout, New York, was completed in 1829. The canal route crossed the Delaware River at Lackawaxen, and there the barges were ferried across the current on cables. However, this crossing often bottlenecked commerce on the canal. The crossing could not be made when the river ran high. Ice jams and floods periodically wrecked the towpath on the New York side. The log-rafting industry was at its height, and the huge rafts often crashed into the ferrying canalboats, sparking fistfights and lawsuits. By 1845 the operators of the D&H Canal realized that an alternative had to be found.

The canal firm consulted John A. Roebling, a German-born engineer who was making a name for himself building bridges in Pittsburgh. Roebling's innovative solution to the Lackawaxen crossing was to build the canal above the water.

The bridge was completed in 1849. Steel suspension cables, eight inches in diameter, were spun by hand at the site and strung between Lackawaxen, Pennsylvania, and Minisink Ford, New York. Conventional construction would have required five stone piers, but Roebling's suspension design needed only three. There was plenty of room for timber rafts and ice flows to pass beneath.

Suspended from the cables, atop the stone piers, was the canal itself, a channel 548 feet long, 6 feet deep, and 20 feet across. The bridge was capable of supporting 3,780 tons. Canal barges loaded with coal, weighing 130 tons, routinely crossed the bridge at Lackawaxen until 1898.

Competition from railroads eventually made the canal operation unprofitable. In 1898 the D&H Canal Company sold the Lackawaxen bridge. The water was drained and the wooden canal trough dismantled. The bridge was used as a road crossing, first for horse and buggy, later for automobiles, until 1979. A succession of private owners collected tolls at the crossing. Finally bankrupt, in 1979, the last of these owners abandoned the bridge. The National Park Service acquired the old bridge as part of the Upper Delaware National Scenic and Recreational River and closed it to traffic.

The bridge at Lackawaxen is a National Historic Landmark. When walking across the bridge, one notices that the wooden-plank decking sways and bounces. Yet the strength of the bridge is undiminished; pedestrians and automobiles hardly have begun to tax the piers, cables, and fittings installed by John Roebling 130 years ago. Engineering students are frequently seen inspecting the bridge, as if on a pilgrimage to this milestone of their trade.

As part of its canal operations, the D&H Company built a dam across the Delaware just upstream from the Lackawaxen bridge. This dam, 16 feet high, was "constructed in the most approved scientific manner, to secure strength," according to J. Wallace Hoff. The river passed through a chute in the center of the dam, dropping about 8 feet and setting up huge haystack waves. This was always a trouble spot for timber raftsmen and was among the greatest hazards on the Delaware for early recreational canoeists. The dam is long gone, but some of its base timbers can be seen

Roebling Bridge, Lackawaxen. Constructed by John Roebling in 1848, it is the oldest surviving suspension bridge in America. The riffle upstream from the bridge marks the remnants of a dam. Photo courtesy of James M. Staples.

at low water near the Pennsylvania shore just upstream from the bridge.

Zane Grey

The banks of the Delaware do not seem a likely place to inspire legends of the Old West. But it was here at Lackawaxen that Zane Grey wrote most of his 111 books about cowboys and Indians, cavalry and bandits.

Zane Grey was born in Ohio in 1872. He studied dentistry and opened an office in New York City. He longed for the great outdoors, however, and in 1905 with his brother, he built a big white house on the shores of the Delaware at Lackawaxen. Inspired by a visit to the ranch of frontiersman Colonel C.J. "Buffalo" Jones, Grey was struck with the idea of writing popular fiction about the West. Over the next 14 years, at his home in Lackawaxen, Grey turned out, one after another, his tales of the West, including *Riders of the Purple Sage, Desert Gold,* and *The Lone Star Ranger.* More than 100 million copies of his books were sold eventually, and he was claimed to be the most popular author in the world. In 1918 Zane Grey moved to California to assist in the production of many silent and talking movies based on his books. He died in 1939.

Zane Grey's home at Lackawaxen is now maintained as a museum. The treasures and memorabilia collected by Grey, along with his old dentist drill, are on display. Photographs and paintings of western scenery and people, Navaho rugs, western clothes, Grey's manuscripts, letters, and articles are all assembled for perusal by visitors.

The Zane Grey house and museum is located at the Lackawaxen access area, about 500 yards upstream from the old bridge.

The Battle of Minisink

Forty-seven revolutionary militiamen were killed in a skirmish near Lackawaxen on July 22, 1779. For 43 years their unburied bones lay about the forests and fields near the banks of the Delaware.

The Lackawaxen area was wilderness at the time of the American Revolution. The first white settlers came to the area only in 1770. On July 20, 1779, Mohawk War Chieftain Joseph Brandt, fighting on the side of the English, led a party of 27 Tories and 60 Indians on a raid of Minisink (now the Port Jervis area). At least four settlers were killed, and houses and barns were burned down. Lieutenant Colonel Benjamin Tusten, on the American side, made quick plans to follow Brandt's raiders and ambush them. About 120 militiamen were mustered to chase Brandt as he retreated up the Delaware.

On the morning of July 22, Brandt's party began to ford the Delaware River at Lackawaxen. The colonial militiamen waited in hiding, but a rifle discharged accidentally, and the ambush was broken. The battle was on. Most of the Continentals took to the high ground on the New York side of the river. The fighting was fierce and lasted throughout the day, ending only when the colonial soldiers, one at a time, made their way into the forest. Forty-seven American militiamen were killed, while only eight of Brandt's raiders were lost.

Not until 1822, when the publication of Tusten's biography aroused public interest in the skirmish, were the bones of the dead collected and taken to Goshen, New York, for burial. In 1847 the skeleton of a Revolutionary soldier was found near the point where the Lackawaxen River joins the Delaware. These remains are now buried in the Unknown Soldier's grave at St. Mark's Lutheran Church at Lackawaxen, a short walk up the road from the Lackawaxen bridge.

Minisink Battleground County Park is located on County Road 168 about one mile up the hill from Route 97 and the old Lackawaxen bridge. This park, site of most of the fighting in the battle, tells the story of the Battle of Minisink by interpretive displays, self-guided trails, and monuments marking the locations of important events. There are picnic sites with grills, rest rooms, and an interpretive center. There is no camping in the park.

CAMPING AND SERVICES

Camping

This section of the Delaware River is entirely within the Upper Delaware National Wild and Scenic River. Virtually all the land adjacent to the river is privately owned, and camping is not allowed without specific permission of the landowner. There are, however, several excellent campgrounds operated by some of the canoe outfitters.

1. Bob and Rick Landers' (Box 376, Narrowsburg, New York 12764, 914/252–3925) operates a large campground on a high wooded bluff at Mile 290.2 just north of the Narrowsburg Bridge. This campground has tent and lean-to sites, modern sanitary facilities with showers, a camp store, and firewood.

2. White Water Canoes (Route 97, Barryville, New York 12719, 914/557–8178) runs a small campground with lean-tos right on the riverbank at Mile 278.5.

3. Bob and Rick Landers' Minisink Ford Canoe Base and Campground with lean-tos and tent sites is located on the river at Mile 275.7.

4. Kittatinny Canoes (P.O. Box 95, Barryville, New York 12719, 914/557–8611/6213) operates Pine Grove Campgrounds with tent sites at Mile 275.8 on the river.

5. Indian Head Canoes (21 Ryerson Avenue, Newton, New Jersey 07860, 914/557–8777) has a campground with its canoe base on the river at Mile 275.6.

6. Kittatinny Campgrounds (P.O. Box 95, Barryville, New York 12719, 914/557–8611) is operated by Kittatinny Canoes and has tent sites and lean-tos on Route 97, accessible from the river at Mile 275.4.

Canoe Liveries

1. Bob and Rick Landers' (Box 376, Narrowsburg, New York 12764, 914/252–3925), established in 1955, is one of the giants of Delaware River canoe liveries with over 1,000 canoes and other river craft. Landers' operates its base at Narrowsburg just upstream from the bridge and provides portage with its own vehicles or a car shuttle service. Landers' sponsors an annual "Dash and Splash" race in May.

2. White Water Canoes (Route 97, Barryville, New York 12719, 914/557–8178) rents canoes from its campground on Route 97, 1.1 miles north of the Lackawaxen bridge.

3. Bob Landers' main base is located at Ten-Mile River Lodge, 4 miles south of Narrowsburg on New York Route 97. Ten-Mile River Lodge is located some distance from the river, but portage is available to all major access points on the upper Delaware.

4. J&J Restaurant and Canoe Landing (Box 136, Narrowsburg, New York 12764, 914/252–6824) rents Coleman, Grumman, Mitchi Craft, and Alumi Craft canoes from its New York Route 97 base, .1 mile north of the Lackawaxen bridge.

5. Bob and Rick Landers' Minisink Ford Canoe Base and Campground, with portage available to all major access points on the upper Delaware, is located on New York Route 97, 2.2 miles north of Barryville.

6. Indian Head Canoes (21 Ryerson Avenue, Newton, New Jersey 07860, 914/557–8777; reservations hotline: 201/579–1616) has a canoe base on New York Route 97, 2.1 miles north of Barryville.

7. Kittatinny Canoes (Box 95, Barryville, New York 12719, 914/557–8611), established in 1952 and one of the largest

canoe outfitters on the Delaware, operates a base at its Kittatinny Campground on New York Route 97, 1.9 miles north of Barryville. Portage is available to every river access area on the upper Delaware.

8. Barryville Kayaks and Canoes (Cedar Rapids Inn, Route 97, Barryville, New York 12719, 914/557–6158) rents kayaks and canoes at the Cedar Rapids Inn, at the head of Big Cedar Rift, on New York Route 97, 1.7 miles north of Barryville.

9. Eberz-Shohola Canoes (Shohola, Pennsylvania 18458, 717/559–7575) has canoes for rent at Shohola Campgrounds, just north of the Barryville-Shohola Bridge in Pennsylvania.

Other Services

The community of Narrowsburg is discussed more fully in the features section of the previous chapter. No major roads come near the Delaware for 10 miles between Narrowsburg and Minisink Ford, and there are no commercial services in that area. Other services are indicated below:

Bob Landers' Ten-Mile River Lodge and Restaurant (Narrowsburg, New York 12764, 914/252–3925) is located on New York Route 97, 4 miles south of Narrowsburg. Portage is available to and from the river.

278.5 Minisink Ford, New York. Spring House Restaurant, affiliated with White Water Canoes.

277.5 Minisink Ford, New York. J&J Restaurant and Canoe Landing.

277.4 Lackawaxen, Pennsylvania. The Lackawaxen General Store is up the road to the bridge on the left.

277.4 Minisink Ford, New York. The Inn at Minisink Ford, located at the Roebling Bridge access.

275.7 Minisink Ford, New York. Bob Landers' Minisink Ford Restaurant, associated with Bob Landers' Canoe Rentals and Campground.

275.2 Barryville, New York. The Cedar Rapids Inn, located on the banks just above the Big Cedar Rift (affiliated with Barryville Kayaks and Canoes). Cedar Rapids Inn sponsors events such as arts and crafts fairs, bluegrass music festivals, and clambakes. For information call 914/557–6158.

Barryville to Port Jervis

The white water of the preceding section continues, though with somewhat less frequency. Shohola Rift, one of the most challenging rapids on the river, and Mongaup Rift, with exceptionally high haystacks, are rated as Class II; about 15 rapids rated at less than Class II also test canoeists' abilities. This section is not suitable for beginners.

A highlight of this area is Hawks Nest, where the Delaware passes dramatically between high cliffs on either side of the river. There are only two islands in this section: Cherry Island at Mile 259 and Mongaup Island at Mile 262.

New York Route 97 parallels the river on the left bank the entire distance between Barryville and Port Jervis. There are no significant towns except for Port Jervis and Matamoras at the end of this section. The Erie Railroad runs very close to the river on the Pennsylvania bank, while the Delaware and Hudson Canal once paralleled the New York bank.

The river continues through the Appalachian Plateaus geophysical province. Shale and sandstone bedrock is exposed prominently in several places, most notably at Hawks Nest. The banks are mostly heavily forested until the urbanized areas of Port Jervis and Matamoras are approached.

This river section is part of the National Scenic River System, under the jurisdiction of the National Park Service. There is only one public access area, at Matamoras, but there are many unim-

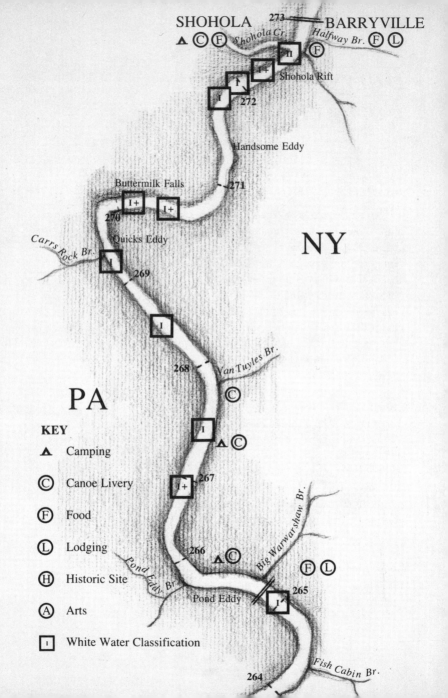

proved access points along New York Route 97. Many private river outfitters operate bases along Route 97 in this area.

RIVER GUIDE

273.0. Pass under the Barryville-Shohola Bridge, constructed in 1941 to replace an older bridge 1/4 mile upstream. The present bridge is at the site of an old ferry crossing. Halfway Brook enters, New York side, just downstream from the bridge. Gravel bars and shallows on the left.

272.9. Enter Shohola Rift (also known as Mitchie Falls), a Class II rapid extending one mile. This is one of the longest and most challenging rapids to be found on the Delaware River. Rapids begin with a drop of about 2 feet over a rock ledge. The clearest channel is on the left.

272.8. Shohola Creek enters, Pennsylvania side, from a steep ravine. Shohola Falls, dropping nearly 100 feet over several ledges, is located on Shohola Creek about 1.5 miles from the Delaware River. The rapids in the Delaware River here are often mistakenly referred to as Shohola Falls. Rapids become more severe with numerous boulders obstructing the channel. The river is deepest in the center here, but canoeists must navigate between boulders.

272.7. The rapids abate for a short distance, then continue. At low water the left side is too shallow to navigate. Cliffs on the left are known as Little Hawks Nest.

272.2. Shohola Rift continues. The main channel, with standing waves to 2 feet, is in the right center. The left side is very shallow at low water. There is a wide rock ledge along the left bank just downstream from the end of Shohola Rift. This is a good place to pull over and bail canoes of the water gained while passing through the rift.

271.9. The final falls of Shohola Rift, at this point a Class I rapid, over boulders and ledges.

271.8. Enter Handsome Eddy. Slow water for one mile.

270.8. Center and left of the river is very shallow. At low water numerous boulders protrude in a line down the middle.

270.5. Begin Buttermilk Falls, a Class I + rapid. The main channel is on the left at moderate and low water level. Right side may be too shallow to navigate. Watch for numerous protruding and submerged boulders.

270.2. Buttermilk Falls continues over a series of three ledges. The last drop is by far the most severe. The main current runs from left center to center, but leads directly towards a single submerged boulder in the very middle of the river.

270.0. Enter Quicks Eddy, continuing .5 mile. Camp Tel-Yehudah, a private camp with neat white buildings, is located on the New York bank.

269.7. River makes a right angle turn to the left.

269.4. Carrs Rock Brook enters, Pennsylvania side.

A Class I rapid, dubbed Lost Channel Rift by J. Wallace Hoff in 1892. A few protruding boulders may be a hazard.

The community of Parkers Glen once stood above the railroad on the Pennsylvania bank. Today only a cemetery and a few foundations remain.

268.5. A Class I rapid, no obstructions.

268.2. Parking area along New York Route 97 atop the New York bluff, with picnic tables and trash barrels.

267.8. Van Tuyles Brook enters, New York side.

267.6. Pass under power line marked by red balls. Gravel bars or shallows on the left.

267.4. A Class I rapid without obstructions. Submerged boulders may be a hazard at low water.

266.7. A Class I + rapid in a constriction of the river.

266.0. Wide rock ledges extend into the river from the Pennsylvania bank.

265.8. Pond Eddy Brook enters, Pennsylvania side.

265.2. Big Warwarshaw Brook enters, New York side. A wide gravel bar extends to near the middle of the river. There is rough access from New York Route 97 under the trees at the upstream end of the gravel bar.

265.1. Pass under Pond Eddy Bridge, a double-truss steel bridge built in 1926. A suspension bridge was built .5 mile upstream in the early 1870s but was washed away in the Pumpkin Flood of 1903, in which the banks and islands of the Delaware were littered with hundreds of pumpkins once floodwaters had receded.

The once thriving community of Pond Eddy is on the Pennsylvania bank. This was the center of the local bluestone slate industry, and the village was once called Flagstone.

264.9. Rough access from New York banks. Very shallow on the left; many boulders protrude from the river.

264.5. A Class I rapid, with protruding and submerged boulders across the river. An abandoned eel weir on the left may be a hazard at low water.

264.3. Pass under a cable crossing. Fish Cabin Brook enters, New York side.

263.6. A roadside picnic table and trash disposal on Route 97 above the New York bank.

263.3. Enter Stairway Rift, a Class I+ rapid. Ledges along the Pennslylvania banks are in the configuration of a staircase, giving this rapid its name. The rift extends .2 mile as a series of ledges with the main channel on the left.

263.0. Stairway Brook enters, Pennsylvania side.

262.7. Enter Knights Eddy, also called Dickersons Eddy; slow-moving water continues .8 mile.

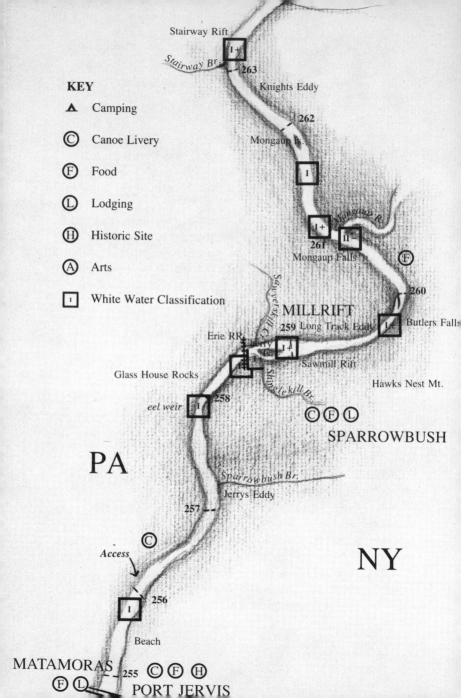

Mongaup Rift. Riding the haystacks. Photo courtesy of James M. Staples.

262.1. The river is bounded on both sides by slabs of shaley bedrock.

262.0. Upstream end of Mongaup Island, which extends .2 mile. The channel on either side is clear, with the main current on the left.

261.9. A Class I rapid is caused by an abandoned eel weir at the downstream end of Mongaup Island.

261.0. The Mongaup River enters, New York side. Enter Mongaup Falls, also known as Mitchels Falls, a Class II− rapid. Ledges and shallows extend from the New York bank, with the current pressed against the Pennsylvania shore. The rapid begins with a boulder ledge, then funnels into a chute where some of the highest standing waves to be found on the Delaware are formed. The channel through the chute is clear, but canoes will almost surely take on water in the three-foot haystacks.

260.0. River bends sharply to the right. A large gravel point bar, known as Butlers Island, has developed on the right side.

Enter Butlers Falls, a Class I+ rapid. The current flows very near the left shore without obstructions; standing waves 2½ feet high make for a wild ride. Rock ledges extend from the left.

Hawks Nest Mountain rises steeply from the river on the New York side. A drive along New York Route 97 over Hawks Nest Mountain is spectacular.

This area was known as the "cellar hole" to timber raftsmen because of the 250-foot sheer cliffs on the left. The cellar hole was a trap for rafts in high water, and raftsmen struggled to keep their crafts as close as possible to the Pennsylvania side to avoid being dashed on the New York rocks.

In the 1800s the Delaware and Hudson Canal ran 40 feet above the river here against the cliffs. Few traces remain. (See the features section of this chapter.)

259.9. Enter Long Track Eddy. The Erie tracks run along the Pennsylvania bank.

259.7. Hay Rock, so called because a ferry hauled hay here for a nearby farm, stands prominently at the base of the New York cliffs.

258.9. Upstream end of Cherry Island (also known as Sawmill Rift Island), which extends .2 mile. The main channel flows right of the island in a Class I + rapid, with the best passage in the center of the channel. The left channel is shallow but passable at moderate water level. There is a Class I rapid with standing waves to 1½ feet at the downstream end of the left channel. Shinglekill Brook enters the left channel.

258.7. Downstream end of Cherry Island. Enter Sawmill Rift, also known as Sawyers Falls, a Class I + rapid. At low water there are numerous submerged and protruding boulders, with shallows extending from the downstream end of the island. The best passage, with standing waves to 2 feet, is in the center of the channel.

The little community of Millrift, Pennsylvania, is very close to the water on the right. A ferry operated here in the last century.

Sawyerskill Creek (known also as Bushkill Creek) enters, Pennsylvania side.

Sawmill Rift was celebrated in verse by Robert "Boney" Quillan, a raftsman-poet of the nineteenth century:

> We sailed around Old Butler's,
> And little did we fear;
> Until we came to Sawmill Rift—
> And slammed against the pier.

258.4. Pass under a bridge carrying the Erie Railroad. First built as a wooden structure in 1850, the bridge was replaced later by the present steel span. A wide gravel beach on the New York shore, just downstream from the railroad bridge. Sawmill Rift ends in a Class I rapid.

258.3. A cliff known as Glass House Rocks rises from the water on the Pennsylvania side. In the early 1800s a plate glass factory operated atop the cliffs. This rock formation is also known as Elephant Feet Rock.

257.9. An active eel weir extends across the river. Canoeists should stay as close to the Pennsylvania shore as possible. There is an abandoned weir immediately downstream from the active one. A Class I rapid flows between the Pennsylvania shore and eel weirs without obstructions. A broad gravel bar extends from the New York bank.

257.2. Enter Jerrys Eddy, a slow stretch of water extending one mile. Sparrowbush Brook enters, New York side.

256.1. Matamoras access area, Pennsylvania side. Maintained by the Pennsylvania Fish Commission. Provides a wide paved ramp, ample parking, sanitary facilities, trash disposal, and fresh water.

255.7. A series of rock ledges extend from the New York bank almost across the river. There is a Class I rapid with standing waves to 1½ feet along the Pennsylvania shore.

255.3. Port Jervis Municipal Beach, New York side.

254.8. River widens and becomes quite shallow, with a moderate riffle over the gravel bottom.

254.7. Pass under the Mid-Delaware Bridge, constructed in 1939. The communities of Port Jervis, New York, and Matamoras, Pennsylvania, stand at opposite ends of the bridge. (See the features section of this chapter.)

FEATURES

Delaware and Hudson Canal

Unlike Pennsylvania's Delaware Canal and New Jersey's Delaware and Raritan Canal, which parallel the Delaware River below Easton and are preserved in state parks, the Delaware and Hudson Canal remains only in traces along its course between Honesdale, Pennsylvania, and Rondout, New York. Finding and retracing segments of the old D&H Canal can be an exciting adventure.

Construction on the Delaware and Hudson Canal began in 1827 to enable shipment of Pennsylvania mountain coal to the tidewater Hudson River and New York City. The first barge passed through in 1829, followed by an almost endless stream of commerce until 1898 when the D&H Canal finally succumbed to competition from the railroads. There were three sections to the D&H Canal: the Lackawaxen section, which paralleled the Lackawaxen River from Honesdale to Lackawaxen; the Delaware section, between Minisink Ford and Port Jervis; and the Neversink section, between Port Jervis and Rondout on the Hudson.

The Delaware section began where the canal crossed the river between Lackawaxen, Pennsyslvania, and Minisink Ford, New York. Initially, the D&H Canal Company constructed a dam to impound the Delaware River so that barges could be towed across the river upstream of the dam. This method, however, was rife with failure, frustration, and lawsuits. Extreme variations in water level, ice flows, and collisions with timber rafts forced an innovative solution upon the canal company. In 1848 the Delaware suspension aqueduct, designed by John A. Roebling, was constructed to carry canal barges over the river at Lackawaxen. This remarkable bridge stands today as the most prominent remaining feature of the D&H Canal.

Most of the way between Minisink Ford and Port Jervis the D&H Canal paralleled the Delaware River and was separated from it only by a stone berm. Today New York Route 97 between Minisink Ford and Barryville is built directly upon the canal right-of-way. In numerous places the carefully laid stone walls that originally carried the canal can be seen underlying the modern highway. The canal route and New York Route 97 likewise coincide in several segments between Barryville and Port Jervis. Near the entrance to the modern Barryville-Shohola Bridge, a historical marker identifies the location of a D&H Canal dry dock. The remains of two lift locks can be discovered also in this vicinity.

Between Barryville and Port Jervis old stonework of the D&H Canal can be seen occasionally along the river. At the Mongaup River, the canal passed through the largest of four aqueducts between Lackawaxen and Port Jervis. Mongaup Village, today just a name on a map, was an important center of canal activity with a dry dock, company buildings, and several canal control facilities. One of the best preserved lift locks stands just a few feet from the river a short way downstream from the Mongaup River.

The course of the D&H Canal through the treacherous Hawks Nest was a considerable engineering feat. Though only traces remain, the canal clung to the New York cliffs atop a 40-foot-high hand-laid stone wall. Butlers Lock, just at the sharpest bend in the river, controlled access to this section of the canal. The foundation of the locktender's house and traces of the stone walls of the canal berm are all that remain today.

Between Cherry Island and the Sawmill Rift railroad bridge the D&H Canal maintained another operations center. This location, known as Bolten Basin, was the scene of the worst of many calamities to befall the Delaware and Hudson Canal. In October 1882 two heavily loaded Erie Railroad flatcars crashed through the iron bridge spanning the canal. Several more cars in the train followed, dragging with them their cargoes, telegraph poles, and the remains of the bridge. The train landed squarely in the canal, forcing its closure for an extended period.

Precariously perched next to the Delaware River, the D&H Canal between Lackawaxen and Port Jervis was especially vulnerable to minor disasters. Frequently the retaining wall would break, draining the canal into the river and stranding commerce.

In the event of such emergencies, special repair scows were on 24-hour standby duty. These boats had right-of-way over all other barges and carried workmen with equipment and materials to repair any damage. In several places guard locks could be closed in order to localize drainage from the canal.

Even with these precautions, serious mishaps occurred. On August 5, 1885, a strong northeast storm dumped heavy rain on the Port Jervis area, flooding the D&H Canal. The numerous waste weirs, designed to vent excess water, were filled with brush and driftwood. At the mouth of Shinglekill Brook, at Bolten Basin, the canal wall breached. Several canalboats became caught in the surge and wedged together near the break, temporarily stemming the tide. But water continued to flood the canal, and a second breach opened a thousand feet upstream from the first. Two hundred feet of canal bank was washed away. Six canalboats were destroyed, and fourteen others were damaged.

The D&H Canal ultimately became unprofitable; on the other side of the river, the New York and Erie Railroad commanded more and faster traffic, and revenue from the shipment of coal on the canal declined steadily in the last half of the nineteenth century. To make up the loss the canal company encouraged excursions on the canal. Tourists and sightseers could take specially outfitted barges up the canal into the scenic Delaware valley. Excursion boats did indeed become popular, but they only postponed the inevitable. In 1898 the D&H Canal was abandoned. Early recreational canoeists paddled along, in the words of J. Wallace Hoff, with "the ever attendant noise of horns and shoutings, together with the choice vocabulary of captains and mule drivers"; today canoeists witness only traces and memories of the Delaware and Hudson Canal.

The New York and Erie Railroad

The rails run close to the river all the way from Hancock to Tusten, where they cross to Pennsylvania at Ten-Mile Rift. From there the tracks closely parallel the Delaware to Sawmill Rift, where the river is spanned by a heavy steel bridge, then continue into Port Jervis and points south. Occasionally a long freight rumbles by, breaking the river's solitude or shaking campers like an earthquake. For the first 75 miles of the Delaware River, canoeists are never far from the New York and Erie Railroad.

In 1825 the Erie Canal opened the American Midwest via its route between the Hudson River at Albany and Lake Erie. It wasn't long before entrepreneurs realized that steam locomotives would someday be faster, more efficient, and more profitable. Plans were unveiled in 1835 for the construction of a railroad from New York City to the shores of Lake Erie, a distance of more than 400 miles, and an enormous undertaking, both physically and financially.

The president of the New York and Erie Railroad had promised that trains would be running to Port Jervis before 1848, and he was a man to keep his word. But it wasn't until the last day of 1847 that the first locomotive arrived in Port Jervis. The locomotive—called the "Eleazar Lord"—and two flatcars carrying dozens of dignitaries were moved into position east of the Neversink River for a triumphant entry into the village. But the tracks had not yet been laid over the Neversink trestle. Well after dark the trainmen, together with local citizens, worked rapidly to get the track in place. A few minutes before 11:00 P.M. all but one piece had been laid, and that rail had to be cut to fit. At only 17 minutes to midnight on December 31, 1847, the rails to Port Jervis were finally completed. The little train chugged into town to begin a grand party.

From Port Jervis the New York and Erie Railroad was to wind north along the Delaware River. Compared to the south bank, the north bank of the Delaware River is quite gentle; however, this side was already occupied by the Delaware and Hudson Canal. By action in the state legislature and courts, the D&H Canal Company pre-empted the railroad from occupying the same bank. So the Erie right-of-way had to be carved out of the rock cliffs on the Pennsylvania side of the river, the railroad crossing the river just above Glass House Rocks near Sawmill Rift. In some places workmen were suspended in baskets from the cliffs. They drilled blast holes in the rock and were hauled to safety after the fuse was lighted.

There was a good deal of animosity between the railroad construction crews and the canal bargemen on the opposite bank. There were countless brawls, and it was not unheard-of for shots to be fired across the river. Railroad crews learned to time their powder blasts with the passage of canal barges, so that the barges and their occupants were showered with rocks and dust. In spite of all this, railroad construction progressed rapidly, and Binghamton, New York, was reached by the end of 1848. Finally, in 1851, the railroad was completed to Dunkirk, New York, on Lake Erie: the East Coast and the American interior were linked.

Since the time of the Roman Empire, wagon axles were made a standard 4 feet 8½ inches long, allowing the wheels to follow the same ruts in the road. The first railroads in England followed this tradition, as did most of the early lines in the United States. But the builders of the New York and Erie Railroad favored a 6-foot gauge to allow heavier traffic and to deter competition from standard gauge roads. In its first decades specially designed Erie locomotives ran between New York, up the Delaware Valley, to Dunkirk on rails 6 feet apart. Inevitably, and at great expense, the Erie standardized its track to be compatible with the equipment and lines used in the rest of the country.

The early days of railroading on the New York and Erie were hazardous. The telegraph had not yet been invented, so there was no effective way to communicate activity along a line. Lapses in communication often resulted in disaster. The worst crash occurred during the Civil War, when a train carrying 800 Confederate prisoners in 19 wooden freight cars slammed head-on with a locomotive hauling 50 cars of coal. Seventy-five souls perished in the wreck. Their remains were buried in a common grave along the tracks in Shohola. In April 1868 at Parkers Glen, several derailed passenger cars plunged off the cliffs to the rocks along the river where they burst into flames. Forty passengers were killed and another 75 injured. Terrible wrecks also occurred at Shohola, Millrift, and Bolten Basin.

Many of the towns and hamlets along the upper Delaware grew around the New York and Erie Railroad. Hancock, Lordville, Long Eddy, Hankins, Callicoon, Narrowsburg, Lackawaxen, Shohola, Millrift, and Port Jervis grew or survived because of their location by the tracks. Each of these towns and hamlets boasted a depot, many of which remain standing.

The New York and Erie tracks, now operated by Conrail, have been upgraded to modern standards. There are frequent freight trains and regular passenger service. Occasionally, a great steam locomotive hauling an excursion train rumbles up the Delaware Valley, echoing the whistles and roar heard there for 136 years.

Port Jervis/Matamoras

It may seem paradoxical that a city so far from the sea could be called a port. Yet Port Jervis is accurately named, for it was once an important canalboat basin and layover for replenishing supplies and resting mules. "P.J.", or "Port," is about halfway along the route of the old Delaware and Hudson Canal, which ran between Honesdale, Pennsylvania, and Rondout, New York. The chief engineer behind the canal was John B. Jervis.

Sparse settlement of the Port Jervis area began in the mid-eighteenth century at Carpenters Point, where the Neversink River meets the Delaware. Among these settlers were John Decker and his family. The historic Decker home, known today as Fort Decker, was rebuilt after an Indian raid in 1779. Now owned and maintained by the Minisink Valley Historical Society, Fort Decker is open to the public on an irregular basis.

After the D&H Canal was opened in 1828, the community of Port Jervis began to thrive. In 1851 the Erie Railroad completed its line between Hoboken, New Jersey, and Dunkirk, New York. Port Jervis, which was about halfway along the route, quickly became a commercial center. Port Jervis was very much a railroad town, so with the closing of the canal and decline of the railroads, the city became less vital. The majestic old railroad terminal, abandoned for many years, has been renovated recently and stands only a few blocks from the Mid-Delaware Bridge. With the construction of Interstate Route 84 and the growth of outdoor recreation in the vicinity, the fortunes of Port Jervis have stabilized. Today Port Jervis is a pleasant small city.

The link across the river between Port Jervis and Pike County, Pennsylvania, has always been an important one. Soon after the first settlers arrived, Benjamin Carpenter and Courtright Middaugh began operating scow ferries from Carpenters Point (where the Neversink River meets the Delaware) to the future site of Matamoras. After the construction of the D&H Canal in 1829, the community of Port Jervis began to grow rapidly at its present location, and the Carpenters Point ferry was abandoned. In 1830 Simeon Westfall began operating a ferry upstream from the river bend, and in 1844 one Gabriel Mapes started a ferry service at River Mile 255.3, which docked at present-day Ferry Street, Port

Jervis. The ferry was nothing more than a crude wooden platform 55 feet long and 10½ feet wide. It was guided by an overhead rope and propelled by the force of the current and by poling against the bottom. Oliver S. Dimmick purchased the Mapes Ferry in 1846. Dimmick was proud to advertise that "careful ferrymen are constantly in attendance, and the rates are very low. The large elephant attached to Turner's menagerie was carried over the Delaware River on this ferry in perfect safety."

Like many of the ferry communities along the Delaware River, Port Jervis and Matamoras soon outgrew the slow-moving scows. In 1854 a 40-foot-wide covered bridge, with separate lanes for foot, wagon, and railroad traffic, was completed. Although the railroad was never installed, this bridge served well until 1870, when it was blown off its pilings in a strong gale. A new wire suspension bridge was completed in 1872; three years later an ice gorge lifted this bridge away and carried it downriver. In a mere 68 days a second suspension bridge was erected to replace the first. This bridge lasted until 1903 when it was destroyed in the famous Pumpkin Flood, so-called because of the many pumpkins left along the river after the floodwaters receded. A double-truss iron bridge was completed at the site the following year and was used until 1939 when it was replaced by the modern Mid-Delaware Bridge. All the Port Jervis/Matamoras bridges were privately owned until 1922, when public sentiment forced the sale of the bridge to the state so that it could be operated as a toll-free crossing.

Matamoras, Pennsylvania, immediately across the Delaware from Port Jervis, grew along with Port Jervis and has always been a satellite community. Unlike Port Jervis, however, Matamoras is laid out in blocks separated by streets and alleys.

There are many services available and accessible to canoeists in Port Jervis and Matamoras. Among these is the Flo-Jean Restaurant in Port Jervis, which has become a local landmark. Located in the old tollhouse at the Port Jervis end of the Mid-Delaware Bridge, Flo-Jean's is renowned for gracious service and excellent cuisine. Inside are many historical photographs of the Port Jervis-Matamoras area; a collection of early American dolls and carriages; antique art; and the old toll panel listing the crossing charges for various vehicles, animals, and people. Other services in the vicinity include the following: 1) Homer's Coffee Shop on East Main Street, Port Jervis; 2) Kentucky Fried Chicken, 33 East Main Street, Port Jervis; 3) Steak House 13, 13th Front Street, Port Jervis; 4) Buffalo Bill's Riverside Hotel, 299 West Main Street, Port Jervis; 5) Sebrandi's Diner, Pennsylvania Avenue, Matamoras; 6) Numerous shops, stores and markets, including a Quick Stop "Midget Market" at the Matamoras end of the Mid-Delaware Bridge; and 7) Two hospitals in Port Jervis.

CAMPING AND SERVICES

Camping

Virtually all the land bounding the river in this section is privately owned. Camping is allowed only with the permission of the landowner. The following are established sites:

1. Shohola Campgrounds (Shohola, Pennsylvania 18458, 717/559–7575) is located along the river just upstream from the Barryville-Shohola Bridge at Mile 273.2. Tent sites are available.
2. Three River Canoes ("Jerry's," P.O. Box 7, Pond Eddy, New York 12770, 914/557–6078) offers campsites for canoeists at its canoe base on New York Route 97, River Mile 267.3.

3. Silver Canoes (37 S. Maple Avenue, Port Jervis, New York 12771, 914/856–7055) has a limited number of riverside tent sites at its Pond Eddy canoe base on New York Route 97, River Mile 265.7.

Canoe Liveries

1. Kittatinny Canoes (Dingmans Ferry, Pennsylvania 18328, 717/828–2700/2338) operates major canoe bases at Pond Eddy (Mile 267.6) and Matamoras (Mile 256.3). Kittatinny Canoes is the oldest and one of the largest liveries on the Delaware, with more than 1,000 Grumman and Old Town canoes for rent. Portage is provided to and from every major access on the upper Delaware River. Recently inner tubes and rafts have been available. Kittatinny Canoes' Pond Eddy base is located on New York Route 97, 2½ miles north of the Pond Eddy Bridge; the Matamoras base is located on the road to Millrift slightly north of the Matamoras access area.

2. Jerry's Three River Canoes (Route 97, Pond Eddy, New York 12770, 914/557–6078) is located at River Mile 267.3, on New York Route 97 about 2 miles north of the Pond Eddy Bridge.

3. Silver Canoe Rentals (37 S. Maple Avenue, Port Jervis, New York 12771, 914/856–7055) uses its Pond Eddy campground as a canoe base. Located at River Mile 265.7, ½ mile north of the Pond Eddy Bridge on New York Route 97.

4. Curt's Sport Shop (Route 97, Sparrowbush, New York 12780, 914/856–5024) is located at the intersection of New York Routes 97 and 42. Offers canoe rentals and fishing advice.

5. Bob and Rick Landers' Delaware River Canoe Trips, (Box 376, Narrowsburg, New York 12764, 914/252–3925), a giant of Delaware River outfitters, keeps canoes for rent at its restaurant The Dock in Sparrowbush, New York, intersection of New York Routes 97 and 42.

6. Bob and Rick Landers' (Box 376, Narrowsburg, New York 12764, 914/252–3925) operates a canoe base near the Matamoras access area, River Mile 256.1. Portage is available to most access areas on the upper Delaware.

7. Indian Head Canoes (21 Ryerson Avenue, Newton, New Jersey 07860, 717/491–2277; reservations hotline: 201/579–1616) rents canoes and kayaks from a base near the Matamoras access area. Portage is available to Indian Head's two other bases and major access points.

Other Services

273.0 Shohola, Pennsylvania. Neena's Italian Food, serving breakfast, lunch and dinner.

273.0 Barryville, New York. Rebers Motel and Restaurant is located at the end of the Barryville Bridge. Cindy's Coffee Shop stands on the opposite side of Route 97.

272.7 Barryville, New York. Soda and ice are available at a gas station.

265.1 Knights Eddy, New York. The Millbrook Inn, featuring "home cooking," is located at the intersection of New York Route 97 and the Pond Eddy Bridge.

265.0 Knights Eddy, New York. Delaware Restaurant and Motel, ice available and outside pay phone.

260.1 Sparrowbush, New York. The Hawks Nest Restaurant is on New York Route 97 one mile up the hill from the Mongaup River.

258.5 Sparrowbush, New York. The community is accessible via a narrow road at the Sawmill Rift railroad crossing. The Alexander Motel, the Hofbrau Motel, the Mighty M Motel, Bob Landers' The Dock Restaurant, Jim's Sport Shop, and Curt's Sport Shop are clustered in Sparrowbush at the intersection of New York Routes 97 and 42.

Port Jervis to Dingmans Ferry

The river changes dramatically as it bends sharply south at Port Jervis. The white water of the previous 40 miles is left behind, and the river becomes wider and generally deeper. Only one rapid, found in the tortuous channels around Quicks Island, presents any real challenge. This section is excellent for beginners.

Port Jervis, New York, and Matamoras and Milford, Pennsylvania, are the main towns to be found in this area. U.S. Route 209 roughly parallels the river on the Pennsylvania side. The New Jersey side is scarcely populated, and virtually no services are available.

The river is deflected south at Port Jervis by the rocks of the Ridge and Valley geophysical province, a band of wrinkled mountains that extends between Vermont and Alabama. The Ridge and Valley Province includes the Kittatinny Mountains in New Jersey and the famous Blue Ridge in Virginia and North Carolina. The Ridge and Valley Province is on the left, while the Pocono Mountain portion of the Appalachian Plateaus Province is on the right.

The islands in this section differ noticeably from the low gravel bars farther upstream. Here the islands rise 15 or 20 feet above the river level on high silty banks. Mature forests have developed on the islands, which are rarely inundated during floods. Towering tulip poplar trees, with an undergrowth of fern, make the islands well worth a stop. These river islands were deposited when the Wisconsin continental glacier melted about 15,000 years ago,

89

swelling the flow with gravel and silt. The river basin itself is filled with debris left by the melting glacier, and bedrock is exposed in very few places.

Most of the land adjacent to the river has been cleared for farming. Some of it is still used as such; however, other areas have reverted to forest. This is an excellent habitat for deer, which are frequently seen along the river's edge on either side. Black bear have been making a comeback in recent years, although they are hardly ever seen. Many species of waterfowl make their nests on the river islands and banks.

This river valley was once inhabited by the Lenni Lenape, or Delaware Indians, and their predecessors. The Indians were here when European settlers first came to the valley, and archaeological exploration has revealed much earlier habitation. In the late eighteenth century the Delawares waged unrelenting war against the settlers. Tom Quick, who lived at Milford, countered with a personal campaign of vengeance which has become a local legend. This area is also known for conservationist Gifford Pinchot, who lived in Milford in the early decades of the present century, and for Dingmans Bridge, at the end of this river section, one of the last private toll bridges in America.

All of the river and adjacent lands in this section are within the Delaware Water Gap National Recreation Area, which is part of the National Park system. There are public access sites at Milford and at Dingmans Ferry, and a few private access points operated by river outfitters.

RIVER GUIDE

254.7. Pass under the Mid-Delaware Bridge, built in 1939, connecting Matamoras, Pennsylvania, and Port Jervis, New York. (See the features section of the previous chapter.) Shallows or gravel bars on left.

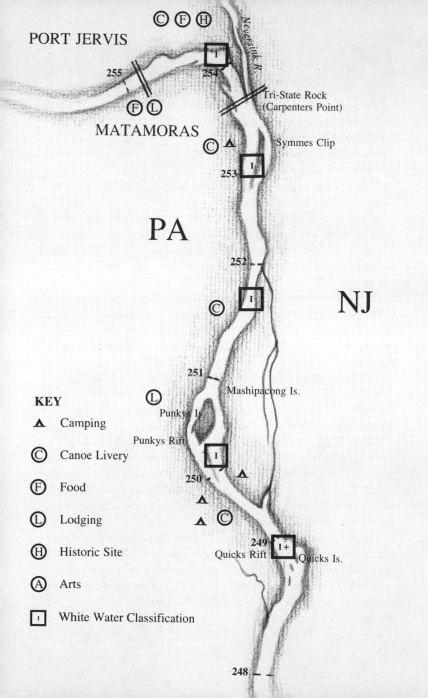

PORT JERVIS

Ⓒ Ⓕ Ⓗ

Neversink R.

255

⊞ 254

Tri-State Rock
(Carpenters Point)

Ⓕ Ⓛ

MATAMORAS

Ⓒ ⟁

Symmes Clip

⊞
253

PA

252

⊞

Ⓒ

NJ

251

Mashipacong Is.

KEY

Ⓛ

Punkys Is.

⟁ Camping

Punkys Rift

⊞

Ⓒ Canoe Livery

250

⟁

Ⓕ Food

⟁

Ⓛ Lodging

⟁ Ⓒ

Ⓗ Historic Site

249

⊞ I+

Ⓐ Arts

Quicks Rift

Quicks Is.

⊞ I White Water Classification

248

254.3. A rock ledge extends halfway across the river from the Pennsylvania side, presenting a Class I rapid. There is clear passage around the left end of the ledge.

254.1. The river makes a right-angle turn to the right. Wide gravel bars on the left.

253.7. Pass under high concrete bridge carrying Interstate Route 84, completed in 1973.

253.6. The Neversink River, one of the principal tributaries of the Delaware, enters on the left. The peninsula at the confluence of the Neversink and the Delaware is called Carpenters Point. Carpenter's Ferry operated between this point and the Pennsylvania shore in the 1700s and early 1800s. Tri-State Rock, a small stone monument with an embedded bronze benchmark, stands on Carpenters Point near the Delaware shore. Tri-State Rock marks the intersection of the boundaries of New York, New Jersey, and Pennsylvania. The little monument is actually located in three states.

253.4. Symmes Clip, with shifting shallows and gravel bars. This area was hazardous for timber raftsmen.

253.1. A Class I rapid with moderate standing waves and a few submerged boulders.

251.9. Upstream end of Mashipacong Island, extending 2.5 miles downstream. At moderate water level the New Jersey channel is dry and visible only as a vegetated pass through the forest.

251.8. A Class I rapid with moderate standing waves flows right to left, then left to right. Submerged boulders near the end of the rapid may be a hazard.

250.8. Upstream end of Punkys Island, in the channel between Mashipacong Island and the Pennsylvania bank. The main channel is left, though the Pennsylvania channel is passable.

250.4. From the main (left) channel a secondary passage cuts diagonally through Punkys Island to the right.

250.2. Enter Punkys Rift, a Class I rapid. There are no obstructions, but canoeists should watch for gravel shallows to avoid scraping the bottom.

249.3. Downstream end of Mashipacong Island.

248.8. Enter Quicks Rift, a Class I+ rapid which eventually diminishes to Class I, one of the trickier rapids to be found on the Delaware. There are no obstructions, but the current flows around gravel bars and Quicks Island. The current, which changes directions suddenly, is capable of pushing canoes into the shore. Sweepers (logs or trees lying in the water) may be a hazard.

At moderate water level the channel near the Pennsylvania shore right of Quicks Island flows between gravel bars with standing waves to 1½ feet. These gravel bars are covered at high water, and this was no doubt the route taken by timber raftsmen.

The main current flows along the New Jersey shore to the left of Quicks Island. There is a fairly narrow channel between gravel bars with standing waves to 2 feet, continuing until deflected by the New Jersey bank, where the channel makes a sudden right turn. Canoeists should try to stay on the inside of the turn to avoid being pushed against the bank.

Quicks Island and Rift are named for the family of Tom Quick, the "Avenger of the Delaware." See the features section of this chapter for more about the adventures of Tom Quick.

248.2. A small stream enters, Pennsylvania side.

247.7. A Class I rapid. Scattered submerged boulders may be a hazard.

247.6. Enter Orchard Eddy, slow water continuing well past Milford.

247.3. Deep Creek enters, Pennsylvania side.

246.9. Sawkill Creek enters, Pennsylvania side. Sawkill Falls, one of the most spectacular cascades in the region, is on this creek about one mile from the Delaware near Grey Towers, the estate of

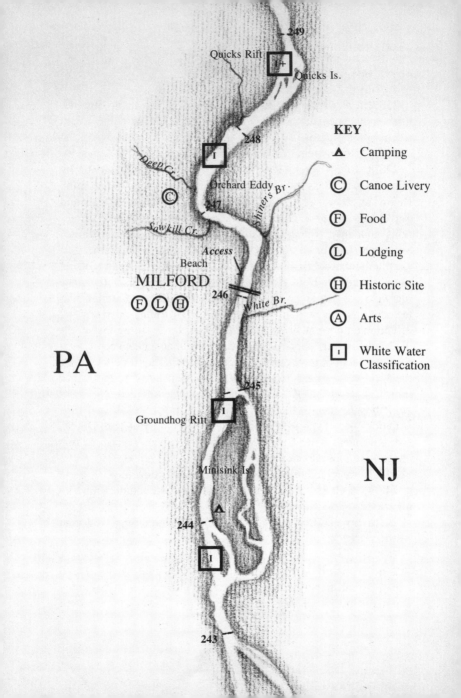

KEY

▲ Camping

Ⓒ Canoe Livery

Ⓕ Food

Ⓛ Lodging

Ⓗ Historic Site

Ⓐ Arts

▢ᵢ White Water
Classification

—249

Quicks Rift   I+   Quicks Is.

—248

Deep Cr.   I

Orchard Eddy   Shiner's Br.

Ⓒ   247

Sawkill Cr.

Access
Beach

MILFORD

Ⓕ Ⓛ Ⓗ   246   White Br.

PA

—245

Groundhog Rift   I

Minisink Is.   NJ

▲

—244

I

—243

Gifford Pinchot, the "father of conservation." (See the features section of this chapter.)

246.5. Shiners Brook enters, New Jersey side.

246.2. Milford Beach, formerly Bob's Beach, on the Pennsylvania side. Maintained for swimming by the National Park Service. A concrete bridge abutment on the Pennsylvania side and its rock counterpart across the river mark the location of the Old Milford Bridge, constructed of steel in 1889. The old bridge has been replaced by the modern concrete bridge slightly downstream. This is the site of Wells Ferry, which plied across the Delaware in the early nineteenth century.

There is a 20-foot-tall metal cylinder standing atop the Pennsylvania bridge abutment, a gauging station to measure the flow of the Delaware River. According to a 1954 ruling of the United States Supreme Court, New York may draw water from the Delaware watershed (mainly from reservoirs on the East and West Branches and on the Neversink River), as long as flow to downstream cities in New Jersey and Pennsylvania is not impaired. The DRBC employs a full-time river master to monitor the river at Milford to ensure adequate downstream flow.

The Milford Beach access area, Pennsylvania side, provides a paved boat ramp, sanitary facilities, drinking water, picnic tables, ample parking, and telephones. The area is maintained by the National Park Service. Access is available from U.S. Route 209.

246.1. Pass under the Milford–Montague Toll Bridge, opened to traffic in 1953. When it was first constructed, this bridge was selected as one of the most beautiful steel bridges in the country. The community of Milford, Pennsylvania, is at the west end of the bridge. (See the description of Milford in the features section of this chapter.)

245.9. White Brook enters, New Jersey side.

245.1. Upstream end of Minisink Island, which extends 2

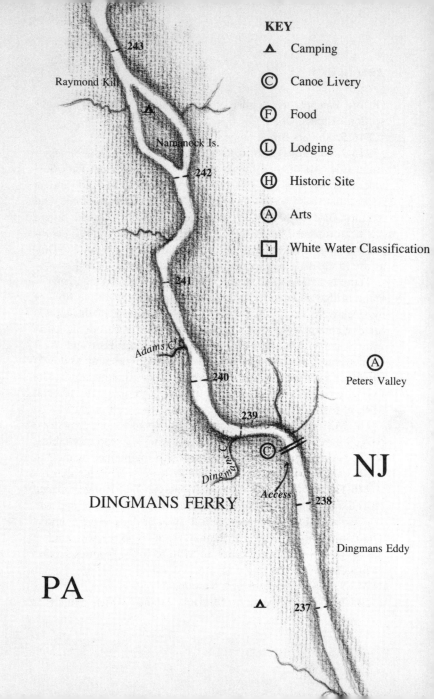

KEY

△ Camping

Ⓒ Canoe Livery

Ⓕ Food

Ⓛ Lodging

Ⓗ Historic Site

Ⓐ Arts

☐ White Water Classification

243

Raymond Kil

△

Namanock Is.

242

241

Adams C.

240

239

Ding mans C.

Ⓒ

Access

238

Ⓐ
Peters Valley

NJ

DINGMANS FERRY

Dingmans Eddy

PA

△ 237

miles. Minisink is the Lenape name for this area. A sizable community of Indians lived on this island when the first settlers arrived.

The main channel runs right of the island and begins with a Class I rapid known as Groundhog Rift. There are standing waves to 1½ feet and no obstructions.

The left channel is passable at moderate water levels. There is a very narrow passage .4 mile into the left channel. The passage leads to the right, then returns to the channel in .8 mile. If the water level is high enough—moderate or above—this winding little passage makes for a good adventure.

243.8. A very narrow channel, passable at moderate water level, leads left from the main channel on the right side of Minisink Island. This passage rejoins the river at the downstream end of Minisink Island. There is a Class I rapid near the channel closest to Pennsylvania shore.

243.4. Downstream end of Minisink Island. There is an exposed gravel bar where the channels rejoin.

242.9. Upstream end of Namanock Island. Channels to the left and right are passable without obstructions.

242.7. Raymond Kill enters, Pennsylvania side.

242.0. Downstream end of Namanock Island. River is slow moving for next 1.6 miles.

240.3. Adams Creek enters, Pennsylvania side. Moderate riffle with no obstructions.

239.1. Dingmans Creek enters, Pennsylvania side. Famous Dingmans Falls and Silver Thread Falls are on this creek about 1.5 miles from the river, accessible via Dingmans Creek Road in Dingmans Ferry.

238.7. Gravel bars and shallows on left.

238.5. Pass under Dingmans Bridge, constructed in 1900. (See the features section of the following chapter.)

FEATURES

Tom Quick and Indian Massacres

According to Ripley's "Believe It Or Not," Tom Quick killed more Indians after he died than the 99 he dispatched during his lifetime. Before this gruesome story may be told, some background is necessary.

When Europeans first arrived in the Delaware Valley, they encountered a sparse group of peace-loving Indians known as the Lenni Lenape. Only 8,000 to 12,000 in number, the Lenni Lenape were scattered in small communities throughout Delaare, eastern Pennsylvania, southern New Jersey, and the upper Delaware Valley. A Lenape community known as the Minsi (people of the stony country) lived in isolation from the rest of the population near what is today Milford. At first the Minsi greeted the white settlers in their traditional manner of hospitality and sharing.

William Penn, who arrived in Philadelphia in 1682, brought with him Quaker ideals. Penn practiced his belief that Indians and whites could live together in harmony. In return, the Lenape regarded Penn as their brother and held him in confidence and respect.

Unfortunately, Penn was present for only four years between 1682 and his death in 1718. Without his guidance, relations with the Indians deteriorated rapidly. The breaking point may have come in 1737, with the infamous Walking Purchase. Two of William Penn's sons convinced the reluctant Lenapes that their father had obtained a deed from the Indians in 1686 that gave the English all the lands within a day-and-a-half walk north from Wrightstown, Bucks County. The Indians presumed this distance to be about 25 miles. The Penns, however, had other ideas. On September 19, 1737, three runners set forth from the starting point, accompanied by horses carrying provisions and two Indian observers. In the allotted day and a half, the athletes had covered 65 miles. The Indians had been cheated sorely; in the words of one Lenape observer, "He run, that's not fair, he was to walk."

Shortly after the outbreak of the French and Indian war, the Lenapes aligned themselves with the French. Over the next several decades, they avenged themselves against whites of all nationalities through a campaign of scalp hunting and plunder. The atrocities, on both sides, were as severe in the Minisink, home of the Minsi, as anywhere in the Lenape nation.

One such incident involved Major Moses Van Campen of Pahaquarry. Van Campen was captured by a band of marauding Lenape in the spring of 1780. But Van Campen and two fellow captives were able to escape one night by cutting their bonds with a knife that Van Campen had secreted. Nine Indians were killed in the escape, and a tenth retreated into the woods. Before the last Indian disappeared, however, Van Campen wounded him in the shoulder with a hatchet. Many years later, in peacetime, this same Indian met Van Campen and identified himself by the hatchet scar on his back.

Another tale concerns the abduction of Sally Decker and her brother, who lived with their parents near the south end of Mashipacong Island. In 1750 the children crossed the river to tend their cows on the other side. Just when they were ready to return home, two Indians appeared out of the woods and snatched the children away. Eight years later, Sally's mother entreated a familiar Indian to help her find her daughter. The Indian said that he would try, and later that summer returned with a squaw at his side. The squaw was Sally, who had learned the ways and language of the

Minsi. Sally said that her brother had married an Indian woman and had not been seen for years. After staying with her parents for a few weeks, and despite their heartrending pleas, Sally went back to the forest, her two sons, and her warrior husband, never to return.

The stage is now set for the legend of Tom Quick. Tom Quick, Sr., a Dutchman, came to the Delaware Valley in 1733. Quick was friendly with the Indians and lived on peaceful terms with them until the outbreak of the French and Indian war. Then, on a cold winter day in 1756, the elder Quick and his two sons, John and Tom, Jr., ventured across the Delaware to New Jersey to inspect their farmlands. There they were ambushed by a party of Lenape. The Quicks were unarmed and attempted to run for safety across the river. Tom Quick, Sr., old and gouty, urged his sons to go on without him. Then, as the boys retreated, the Indians fell upon the elder Quick, killed and scalped him, and took a pair of silver knee buckles from his body. Then and there Tom Quick, Jr., vowed that he would avenge his father's death by never letting any Indian escape from him alive.

Tom Quick's campaign of revenge continued until his death in 1796. He was cunning and merciless in his mission, often befriending Indians and then killing them at an opportune moment. The most famous tale has it that one day while Tom was splitting logs in a clearing, seven Indians came up to him, intent on taking him away. Tom said that he would go, but asked if the Indians would first help him split the last large log. As Tom drove a wedge deeper into the log, he instructed the Indians to pull the log apart at the split with their fingers. When the log was nearly split, Tom quickly knocked the wedge out, and the log snapped shut on the Indians' fingers. Then, at his leisure, Tom dispatched the seven, one at a time.

Another legend has it that Tom once apprehended an Indian family in a canoe. He quickly killed the mother and father, then hesitated as he approached the infant. Any thoughts of mercy were short-lived, however, for Tom said to himself, "Nits make lice," and then killed the baby with his hatchet.

Whenever Tom killed an Indian, he would search the body for his father's silver buckles. One day in a tavern he met an Indian named Mushwink, who had long ago been Tom's friend. Mushwink became quite drunk, began to brag about some of his exploits, and finally produced a pair of silver buckles exclaiming, "Me Tom Quick, me Tom Quick now." Tom grabbed a gun from over the fireplace, but the innkeeper forebade Tom from killing the Lenape in the tavern. Mushwink, realizing what he had done, walked proudly out the door; Tom shot him dead in the street.

When Tom Quick died, his only regret was that he had not killed more Lenape. Upon his death, according to legend, gleeful Indians took pieces of Quick's body to show their brethren that Quick was at last gone. By this demonstration many Indians were infected with smallpox and died, so Tom Quick's vengeance was carried on from his grave.

Some accounts portray Tom Quick as a hero, "the Avenger of the Delaware." Modern authorities regard him as a psychopathic killer. Nevertheless, stories of Tom Quick are told often in the Delaware Valley. Many of the Quick family are buried in the old graveyard nestled amongst the pines near the entrance to Grey Towers. A monument to Tom Quick himself may be found at the intersection of Broad and Sarah Streets in Milford. Interred in the base of this monument is a glass jar containing the remains of Tom Quick. The Tom Quick Inn is also on Broad Street, where for many years a painting of the legendary split log could be seen on the door.

Milford, Pennsylvania

When Abraham Lincoln was shot at Ford's Theater in 1865, his attendants rested his head on a flag hanging from the balcony. This flag, stained with Lincoln's blood, now hangs in a glass case at the Pike County Historical Society's museum in Milford. Located in the attic of the community house at the corner of Harford and Broad Streets, the museum contains a potpourri of items representative of earlier life in Pike County. There are dozens of projectile points of the Lenape and their forebears, old farm tools, early hotel registers, items of Victorian clothing, photo albums, volumes of genealogy, and perhaps most important, a wealth of knowledge in the members and officers of the historical society. The little museum is reminiscent of grandmother's attic, for although the collections are well-organized, they are crammed so tightly together that it is difficult to tell where the arrowheads end and the farm tools begin. The historical society is hopeful of gaining more spacious accommodations.

The community house itself, constructed in 1834, was the original homestead of the Pinchot family. The Pike County Library is also housed here.

According to tradition, Milford was founded in 1733 with the settlement of Tom Quick, Sr. The community was later known as Wells Ferry; the origin of the modern name is not clear. Milford has been a residential and vacation-oriented community since the mid-nineteenth century.

Milford's most famous citizens were Tom Quick, the "Indian Slayer," and Gifford Pinchot, the "Father of Conservation." This heritage aside, Milford is a fascinating place. Sawkill Creek rushes through a glen immediately south of town; the old Metz ice plant, now owned by the National Park Service, is located in this glen on the site of an old mill. There are numerous old inns, churches, and homes about the town, each with its own history.

The physical layout of the Milford community is worthy of interest. Grassy alleyways bisect the blocks between the main residential streets, which are lined with tall shade trees and Victorian homes. The wide sidewalks on Broad Street are made of great slabs of blue slate quarried in the vicinity. Hitching posts remain at intervals throughout the community, although their usefulness ended decades ago.

Milford also meets the needs of modern times, with a supermarket, movie theatre, laundromat, several restaurants, taverns, banks, and lodges.

Milford may be reached best from the Delaware at the National Park Service beach immediately downstream from the confluence of the Delaware and Sawkill Creek, about ½ mile upstream from the new Milford bridge. Take a short walk up the beach road to Route 209, then turn right to Harford Street.

Grey Towers

On a hill above Milford, beside the tumbling waters of Sawkill Creek, stands Grey Towers. The legacy of the science of forestry in America can be traced to these grounds. It was here in the late nineteenth century that young Gifford Pinchot became acquainted with the ways of the forest, and it was from here that Pinchot went on to become the father of American conservation.

Gifford Pinchot was born into a wealthy family in 1865. James Pinchot, Gifford's father, fervently believed that the wise use of natural resources was essential to the nation's welfare. At his suggestion, Gifford decided to become a professional forester. Scientific forestry, however, was unknown in America in the 1800s, so Gifford studied in France. When he returned, he was the first truly professional forester in America and was quickly employed at the Vanderbilt Estate near Asheville, North Carolina. In 1898, Pinchot became chief of the Division of Forestry in the U.S. Department of Agriculture.

Pinchot became known to Theodore Roosevelt, who was himself an ardent student of nature and who admired the principles and practices advanced by Pinchot. When Roosevelt became president, the Division of Forestry was elevated to the U.S. Forest Service; Pinchot remained as chief of the Forest Service until 1910.

Pinchot's philosophy of conservation was guided by the principle that natural resources should be managed for the greatest good of the greatest number in the long run. But there were rivals within the growing conservation movement. Foremost among these was John Muir of California, who advocated protection and preservation of forest lands and other resources lest those remaining fall to wanton consumption. The most notable disagreement between Pinchot and Muir centered on the issue of water supply at Hetch Hetchy, California. More water was needed to fill the demands of the burgeoning population; there were plans to build a great reservoir. Muir argued that the reservoir would destroy valuable resources forever; under Pinchot's philosophy the reservoir would provide the greatest good in the long run. Ironically, the same philosophical battle is being fought today in the backyard of Grey Towers. Advocates of the Tocks Island Dam champion Pinchot's multiple use concept, while preservationists claim that valuable resources will be lost if the dam is built. Today, John Muir's philosophy of preservation is evident in many programs of the National Park Service, while Gifford Pinchot's legacy of management and philosophy of multiple-use guide the U.S. Forest Service.

After his 10 years with the U.S. Forest Service, Pinchot went on to become a professor at Yale. He helped found and was the first president of the Society of American Foresters. Pinchot also served two terms as governor of Pennsylvania (1923–1927 and 1931–1935) and is recalled by many as one of the great governors of that state.

In 1886 James Pinchot built a 41-room mansion on the hill in Milford. This estate, Grey Towers, was Gifford Pinchot's country home until his death in 1946. The 3600 acres surrounding the house were managed according to Pinchot's principles. For a while, Grey Towers was also used as a training facility for Yale forestry students.

In 1963 the Pinchot family donated Grey Towers to the U.S. Forest Service, with President John Kennedy on hand for the dedication. The Forest Service now administers the Pinchot Institute for Conservation Studies at Grey Towers, which is dedicated to the ideals of Gifford Pinchot. The institute is a "think tank" where conservation issues can be analyzed.

Parts of the mansion and grounds are open to the public, with daily summer tours every hour between 10 A.M. and 4 P.M. The estate is notable as a representation of upper-class life at the turn of the century. The mansion also contains exhibits of some of Pinchot's personal collections and memorabilia.

On the opposite side of a field to the south of the mansion, a shaded trail leads to Sawkill Falls. Among the most magnificent of falls along the Pocono front, Sawkill Creek cascades into a steep, narrow chasm. The falls are located on the private property of the Pinchot family, and the area is not maintained by the Forest Service. Visitors are usually permitted to visit the falls with the understanding that private property must be respected.

Grey Towers is located in Milford about one mile from the Delaware River. Go through town on Harford Street, then bear left at the "Y"; the entrance to Grey Towers will be found on the left.

CAMPING AND SERVICES

Camping

1. The river in this section passes through the Delaware Water Gap National Recreation Area. Primitive camping for one night only is permitted on Mashipacong Island (Mile 252 to Mile 249.4), Minisink Island (Mile 245.1 to 243.4), and Namanock Island (Mile 242.9 to 242.0). There are no facilities or maintenance on these islands, but sites have been established by consistent use. Be prepared to rough it. As there is no road access, camping is only among fellow canoeists.
2. Thirsty Deer Campsites, a private campground, is located at Mile 249.8 on the Pennsylvania bank.
3. Kittatinny Canoes operates its River Beach campsites (Box 382, Milford, Pennsylvania 18337, 717/296–7421) at Mile 249.7. There are numerous wooded campsites on the river, each with a picnic table, fireplace, and trash disposal. There are a few lean-tos, modern sanitary facilities, showers, ice, and firewood.
4. Tri-State Canoes (Shay Lane, Matamoras, Pennsylvania 18336, 717/491–4948) operates a riverfront campground at Mile 253.5. Each tent site has a fireplace and picnic table.

Canoe Liveries

1. Tri-State Canoes (Shay Lane, Matamoras, Pennsylvania 18336, 717/491–4948) rents canoes and other river craft for day outings or extended trips. Instruction and trip planning can be provided. Tri-State Canoes' riverfront base is located on Shay Lane, off Rose Lane, in Matamoras, Pennsylvania.

2. Indian Head Canoes (21 Ryerson Avenue, Newton, New Jersey 07860, 201/579–1616; 717/296–8050) operates one of its three canoe bases just north of Milford, Pennsylvania, with access from U.S. Route 209.

3. Pocono Canoe Rental (Route 209, Box 700, Matamoras, Pennsylvania 18336, 717/491–2373) is located on U.S. Route 209 at River Mile 251.6.

4. Kittatinny Canoes (Dingmans Ferry, Pennsylvania 18328, 717/828–2700/2338) operates major canoe bases at its River Beach campsites (River Mile 249.7) and at the Pennsylvania end of Dingmans Bridge (River Mile 238.5). Although it began with only a few boats in 1952, now Kittatinny Canoes is one of the largest liveries on the Delaware River. Grumman and Old Town canoes are available to rent, with portage provided to any access on the upper Delaware. Rubber rafts and inner tubes are also available.

Other Services

There are no commercial services accessible from the river in New Jersey through this section. The communities of Port Jervis, New York, and Matamoras, Pennsylvania, are discussed in the preceding chapter. Milford, Pennsylvania, is discussed more fully in the features section of this chapter.

250.7 South of Matamoras, Pennsylvania. Tourist Village Motel and Village Diner, located on U.S. Route 209.

Dingmans Ferry to Tocks Island

This section is among the longest, in terms of time, in the course of the river. There are a few easy rapids, but slow eddies are the rule. Walpack Bend, the most significant feature here, adds about three miles to the straight line distance. When the wind blows from the southwest, as it often does, vigorous paddling is required to make any headway at all. To attempt the whole reach in a single day requires considerable stamina of muscle and mind.

The river here has a character similar to the immediately preceding section. Islands are large and heavily treed, favored nesting places for many species of waterfowl and other birds. Below Walpack Bend the river marks the western boundary of the Ridge and Valley geophysical province, and exposures of bedrock are seen in several locations. Kittatinny Mountain rises sharply on the New Jersey side. Updrafts along the mountain are used by many species of hawks in their autumn migration south. Birdwatchers flock to this area every fall to witness this spectacle.

The river channel is filled with debris remaining from the continental ice sheet. The rapids, which are not very severe, tumble over glacial deposits of boulders, rather than the bedrock ledges found at Skinners Falls or Foul Rift. Three rapids—Fiddlers Elbow, Mary and Sambo, and one near Depew Island—can be challenging.

The river and adjacent lands are within the Delaware Water Gap National Recreation Area, which is part of the National Park system. U.S. Route 209 roughly parallels the river in Pennsylvania, and the historic Old Mine Road, traditionally the oldest highway in America, approaches the river in several places in New Jersey. There are no substantial communities on either side, and commercial services are limited. The National Park Service maintains six access areas: Dingmans Ferry, at the beginning of this section; Eshback access, Mile 231.6; Bushkill access, Mile 228.2; Depew access, Mile 221.3; Pahaquarry access, Mile 220; and Smithfield Beach access, just upstream from the head of Tocks Island. The private outfitters in the vicinity use the public access areas.

Tocks Island, at the end of this section, is the site of a proposed dam that would impound the Delaware River as far north as Port

Dingmans Bridge, circa 1910. The scene is little changed today. Photo courtesy of Pike County Historical Society.

Jervis. Plans for the dam have been shelved but may be dusted off in the future.

The ease of access, its suitability for novices, the magnificent scenery and wilderness make this section among the most popular in the river. Canoe traffic can be heavy!

RIVER GUIDE

238.5. Pass under Dingmans Bridge. (See the features section of this chapter.)

Dingmans Ferry public access area, Pennsylvania side, is operated by the National Park Service (until 1978 operated privately by Kittatinny Canoes), with plenty of parking, a wide gravel ramp, sanitary facilities, telephones, and trash disposal. On the New Jersey bank there is a steep, unimproved access, formerly used by canoeists and fishermen unwilling to pay Kittatinny a fee for use of the ramp on the opposite bank.

Dingmans Eddy, wide and slow, continues 1.6 miles. In rafting days Dingmans Eddy was a stopping place second in importance only to Upper Black Eddy.

237.0. A moderate shallow riffle across width of river; submerged rocks may be a hazard.

236.5. Another easy riffle.

236.3. Channel on left presents a Class I rapid. The middle and right of river is shallow and crowded with submerged aluminum-streaked rocks. The deepest channel from here to Walpack Bend tends to be nearer the New Jersey bank.

236.2. Hornbeck Creek enters, Pennsylvania side.

235.4. Easy riffle; best passage on left side.

234.9. Shapnack Island (formerly Bacon Egg Island). Main channel on the left; the channel to the right of the island is pass-

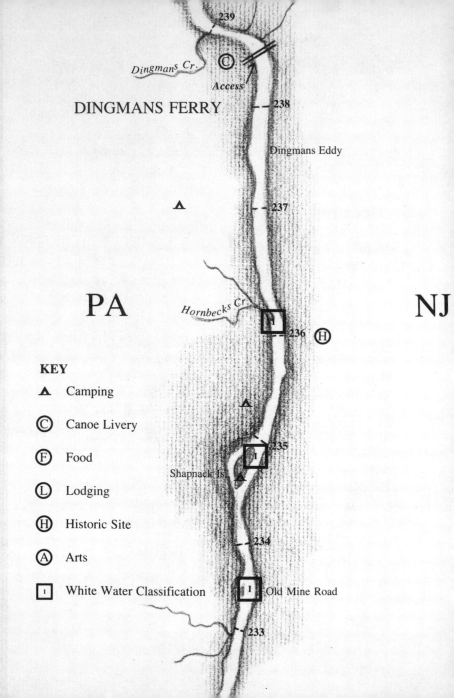

239

Dingmans Cr.

Ⓒ

Access

DINGMANS FERRY

— 238

Dingmans Eddy

▲

— 237

PA

Hornbecks Cr.

NJ

▣ I

— 236 Ⓗ

KEY

▲ Camping

Ⓒ Canoe Livery

Ⓕ Food

Ⓛ Lodging

Ⓗ Historic Site

Ⓐ Arts

▣ I White Water Classification

▲

▣ I — 235

Shapnack Is.

▲

— 234

▣ I Old Mine Road

— 233

able at moderate water level. A Class I rapid; shallow, watch for submerged rocks.

234.4. Downstream end of Shapnack Island; another shallow riffle.

233.5. A small gravel bar near the Pennsylvania shore near the mouth of a small tributary; the right passage is not navigable. There is a short Class I rapid with a clear deep channel near the New Jersey bank.

The river narrows and is quite straight for the next mile. Summer cottages on the New Jersey bluff are among the few not razed in contemplation of the Tocks Island Dam. The Old Mine Road (see description in the features section) parallels the river very closely.

232.0. River widens into a slow pool for the next mile.

231.6. Eshback public access area, undeveloped, with limited parking, maintained by National Park Service.

231.0. Buck Island, a broad gravel bar, in the center of the river. The right channel is marginally passable; left channel is narrower but deep enough.

230.9. Easy riffle at end of island; very shallow near island.

230.6. River turns sharply left, entering Fiddlers Elbow Rift, a Class I rapid with no obstructions and standing waves to 2 feet. The deepest channel is on the right until the river bends right; then the channel is on the left.

230.4. Toms Creek enters, Pennsylvania side.

229.1. River bends slightly right in a long easy riffle; watch for submerged rocks.

228.4. U.S. Route 209 is very close to river for next .4 mile.

228.2. Bushkill public access area, with a boat ramp and limited parking, maintained by Pennsylvania Fish Commission.

227.3. Large cottages and private boat docks on Pennsylvania shore.

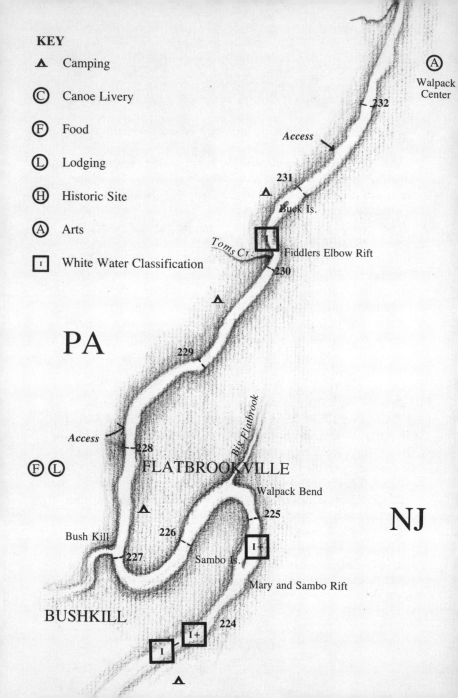

KEY

△ Camping

Ⓒ Canoe Livery

Ⓕ Food

Ⓛ Lodging

Ⓗ Historic Site

Ⓐ Arts

□I White Water Classification

Ⓐ Walpack Center

232

Access

231

△

Buck Is.

Toms Cr

□I

Fiddlers Elbow Rift

230

PA

△

229

Access

228

Ⓕ Ⓛ

Big Flatbrook

FLATBROOKVILLE

Walpack Bend

225

△

226

□I+

Bush Kill

227

Sambo Is.

Mary and Sambo Rift

NJ

BUSHKILL

224

□I+

□I

△

227.0. Bush Kill enters, Pennsylvania side, with broad gravel shallows extending halfway across the river.

226.7. Begin left U-turn of Walpack Bend. Walpack Bend, a great "S" turn in the Delaware, is formed where the river has cut through the hard rocks of Walpack Ridge. The bend is really a small water gap, geologically similar to the Delaware Water Gap 16 miles downstream. Rocks nearby yield many fossils.

225.4. Big Flatbrook, "a trout stream of no mean reputation," according to Charles Hine, enters, New Jersey side. A whirlpool in Big Flatbrook near here was known to the Lenape Indians as "Wahlpeck," hence the name of the township. Alternatively, "Walpeek" means "deep water," likewise accounting for the origin of "Walpack." Take your pick.

225.1. Begin the right U-turn out of Walpack Bend as the current increases.

224.6. Sambo Island, a small gravel bar, in the right of the channel.

Enter Mary and Sambo Rift, a Class I+ rapid, beginning with a perceptible drop over .1 mile. Large protruding and just submerged rocks may present a hazard. There is no clear channel, and considerable maneuvering may be required. After a short swift pool the rapids continue, with the channel flowing from left to right over rocks, until ending in 2-foot standing waves at mile 223.9.

223.7. A prominent rock, known as "Van Camp's Nose," protrudes from river on the Pennsylvania side.

223.6. The river constricts in a Class I rapid, with no hazards.

222.8. Pass under high-tension lines.

222.0. Depew Island (formerly Van Campens Island). Left passage is dry at low to moderate water levels. Class I rapid in the narrow right passage makes an "S" turn around the point of island, no obstructions, with standing waves to 2 feet.

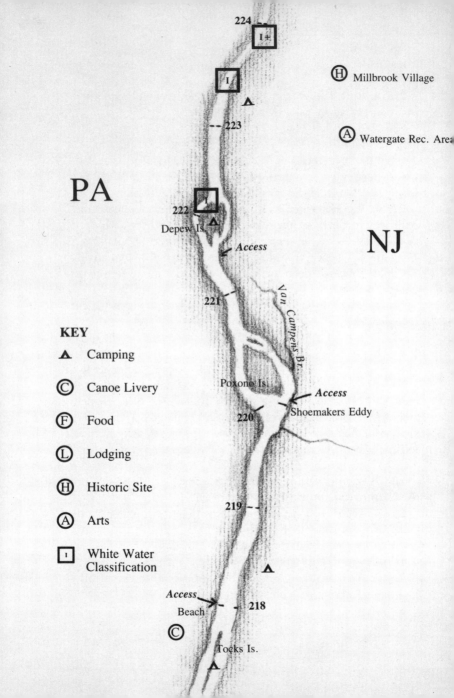

224

I+

H Millbrook Village

I

▲

A Watergate Rec. Area

- - **223**

PA

I

222

▲

Depew Is.

NJ

Access

- - **221**

Van Campens Br.

KEY

▲ Camping

Ⓒ Canoe Livery

Poxono Is.

Ⓕ Food

Access

Ⓛ Lodging

220

Shoemakers Eddy

Ⓗ Historic Site

Ⓐ Arts

I White Water
Classification

- - **219**

▲

Access

Beach

- - **218**

Ⓒ

Tocks Is.

▲

221.6. A great boulder protrudes from the river, Pennsylvania side.

221.3. Depew public access area, New Jersey side; a gravel ramp, unimproved parking, outhouses; maintained by the National Park Service. Access from here to the Watergate Recreation Area (see description in features section) and Van Campens Glen natural area.

220.5. Begin Poxono Island (formerly Mine House Island). The left channel is very shallow and usually impassable; the current is swift in the main channel.

220.0. River becomes very wide (Shoemakers Eddy) immediately downstream of Poxono Island, which is popular with motorboaters.

Van Campens Brook enters from behind Poxono Island, New Jersey side. A short distance up the brook is Van Campens Glen, a protected natural area where the stream cascades through a hemlock ravine. Picnic facilities are available.

Pahaquarry public access area, New Jersey side. There is a steep gravel ramp, limited parking, and water. Maintained by National Park Service.

The Old Mine Road runs atop the New Jersey bluff.

219.4. Traces of a road can be seen in the forest on either side. This is the site of Dimmick's Ferry, a crossing which operated in the nineteenth century.

218.0. Smithfield Beach public access area. Paved ramp, parking, water, sanitary facilities, picnicking, telephones, trash disposal, guarded and roped sand beach. Operated by the National Park Service.

217.9. Upstream end of Tocks Island. Channels on either side are passable with swift current and short riffles, though the left channel is narrower. The Old Mine Road runs very close, New Jersey side. This is the proposed site of the controversial Tocks Island Dam. (See the features section of this chapter.)

FEATURES

Dingmans Ferry

> I have journeyed far, both east and west,
> Far north and south, too, very.
> But the sweetest place amongst all the rest
> Is hill-bound Dingmans Ferry.
>
> The days I've spent among the hills
> Were joyous, free and merry,
> Amongst "veteran" rocks and
> Murmuring hills
> Found but at Dingmans Ferry.
>
> In a vine-clad tavern, near the road,
> Thoughts of the world I bury,
> Such hosts and hostesses you'll find
> Only at Dingmans Ferry.
>
> Then I'll fill my glass—drink to the host,
> And the hostess' cheeks so cherry,
> And to the days I love the most—
> The days at Dingmans Ferry.

In 1735 Andrew Dingman, a Dutchman from Kinderhook, New York, obtained deeds to extensive lands 13 miles above Bushkill and 8 miles below Milford. The vicinity was replete with mill power from the tumbling waters of what became known as Dingmans Creek, and here Andrew Dingman chose to seek his fortune. Indeed, the homestead and environs became known as Dingmans Choice.

Dingmans Choice was in a strategic location for westbound traffic through Culvers Gap and the Old Mine Road in New Jersey. Soon after he arrived, Andrew Dingman constructed a crude rectangular raft to accommodate the growing stream of pioneers desiring to cross the river. The ferry also was used to communicate and trade with the New Jersey side and, when necessary, to escape from marauding Indians. Dingman and his son Andrew II, his grandson Judge Daniel Dingman, and finally Andrew Dingman III operated the little ferry for 101 years.

By 1834 the burgeoning local population demanded a more efficient means of crossing the river. Dingmans Choice and Delaware Bridge Company was chartered that year as a private enterprise to construct and operate a bridge at Dingmans Ferry. A fine wooden bridge was completed in 1836 and was well used until 1847. That year the spring floodwaters of the Delaware washed the bridge at Milford off its piers and carried it crashing downstream into the bridge at Dingmans. Dingmans Bridge was rent into three parts; one section remained on its piers, while the other two were swept away along with the remnants of the Milford Bridge. Andrew Dingman III, who was tolltaker at the time, kept about two hundred pigeons roosting about the bridge; all were lost when the bridge was washed away. The old ferry was called back into service while plans were made to replace the bridge.

The second Dingmans Bridge was completed in 1850. It is believed that this bridge was covered, for the diaries of residents contain accounts of hauling snow into the bridge to make for better passage by horse-drawn sleds. Unfortunately, this bridge too was short-lived. About five years after its completion, a great gale lifted the bridge wholly from its stone foundations and then dropped it into the river. Once again the ferry was hauled out of storage and put into service.

In 1856 a third wooden bridge was constructed on the existing stone piers. Evidently this bridge was poorly constructed or was made from inferior materials, for the structure collapsed and fell into the river in 1862.

Dingmans Ferry, circa 1890. Typical of the many scow ferries that crossed the Delaware in the eighteenth and nineteenth centuries. The abutments of the early Dingmans bridges stand in the background. Photo courtesy of Pike County Historical Society.

Still again the ancient ferry was hauled out to ply the water between Pennsylvania and New Jersey. Until 1875 Andrew Dingman III pulled a 12-foot by 45-foot craft back and forth by an overhead cable. Then the operation was purchased by John W. Killsby who, with his son, operated the ferry until 1900. The ferry was in service 24 hours a day and could be summoned by tolling a bell from the opposite shore.

Nevertheless, the old slow ferry did not match the quickening pace of the times. Dingmans Choice and Delaware Bridge Company sought to raise $15,000 to build a new bridge in 1889, but this effort was not successful. At about this time Dr. J. N. Miller, a Layton physician, avoided ferry delays by pulling himself across the river in a basket suspended from the ferry cable. Dingmans Choice and Delaware Bridge Company, nearly bankrupt, lost the bridge franchise at a tax sale to the Perkins brothers, owners of the Horsehead Bridge Company. The Perkins brothers were in possession of the remnants of a bridge that had crossed the Susquehanna River at Muncie. They hauled three pin-hung wrought-iron trusses from that bridge to Dingmans. New stone piers were built, and the existing embankments raised six feet. The bridge was opened for traffic in 1900, with tolls assessed as follows:

2 horse wagon	25 cents
1 horse wagon	18 cents
horseless carriage	40 cents
horse and rider	10 cents
horse sled	6 cents
footman	2 cents
bicycle	5 cents
tandem	6 cents
cattle	3 cents

As a center of traffic and commerce Dingmans Choice naturally developed into a thriving community. By the 1840s there were numerous dwellings, a school, store, blacksmith shop, and at least one tavern. Dingmans Choice was famous among river raftsmen for its accommodations, and it was a favorite stopping place. By the mid-nineteenth century the village had become identified with the ferry operation, and in 1868, by action of the U.S. Post

White-washed toll house of Dingmans Bridge, River Mile 238.5. One of the last privately-owned toll bridges in America. Photo by the author.

Office became officially known as Dingmans Ferry. In the later decades of the 1800s Dingmans was a favorite place of artists and vacationers. At least half a dozen hotels thrived during this era.

All of the old bridges across this part of the Delaware River were once privately owned. But candidates for local office made political hay out of the tolls; in 1906 Alfred Marbin became the first Republican elected to the state legislature from Pike County in one hundred years, running on a platform of free bridges. Today, the bridge at Dingmans is the only private bridge across the Delaware and one of the last in the country. Dingmans Choice and Delaware Bridge Company, chartered in 1834, continues to accommodate travellers across the bridge between New Jersey and Pennsylvania. Today the toll is 50 cents.

Virtually nothing remains of the village of Dingmans Ferry. The great stone house of Andrew Dingman II, built in 1803, now vacant and boarded up, stands sentinel at the Pennsylvania access to the bridge. At the whitewashed wooden tollhouse there is a bulletin board where notices of local antique shows, church fairs, and community activities are posted. Kittatinny Canoes operates a base behind the old Dingman house, and the National Park Service maintains a large river access just downstream from the bridge. Between the National Park Service boat ramp and the bridge is a wide grassy lawn shaded by aged tulip poplars. Here one may sit for lunch or rest "amongst 'veteran' rocks and murmuring hills . . . found but at Dingmans Ferry."

Old Mine Road

Along the way from Dingmans Ferry to Walpack Bend, canoeists occasionally may see a lone car driving along a road atop the bluff on the New Jersey side. The car makes slow progress, bumping and dipping through potholes, leaving a cloud of dust in its wake. "What a terrible road!" one may think. A scramble up the bank confirms this impression. The road in places is not wide enough for two cars to pass. Although once paved, the road's asphalt is broken and, in places, completely gone. Potholes more like chasms string on endlessly and often completely engulf the right-of-way in a trench a foot or more deep. A handful of rustic cottages perch between the road and the river; their presence seems the only possible purpose for the road's existence. With a shrug of the shoulders, the canoeist may conclude that as the cottages disappear, the old road too will fade away. (Some cottages are in the final stages of disrepair; others nearby have been razed by the federal government in anticipation of the Tocks Island Lake.)

But this rugged road has survived a long time. It was here before the cottages, before the canals to the north and south, before rafts loaded with timber were floated to Philadelphia, before the formation of the United States, before the colonies were ruled by the King of England, before any other road of its length existed in North America. This narrow, potholed, dusty road, known as the Old Mine Road, is considered traditionally the oldest highway in America.

It is generally believed that the road was used by the earliest settlers to haul copper ore from mines near the Delaware Water Gap one hundred miles north to Kingston on the Hudson River. The mines were worked by Dutch pioneers before 1700 at least, and it is possible that the road was first developed by that hardy group. The miners evidently did not know where the flow of the Delaware led to, and in any event Philadelphia itself was of no commercial significance at the time. There was surely more interest in bringing the fruits of their toil to their Dutch brethren at New Amsterdam (New York).

In 1730, two agents from Philadelphia tramped through the wilderness to investigate rumors of a settlement and mines far upriver. They found at Pahaquarry a thriving and long-established community. In 1787, when the first mines had been long abandoned, one investigator inquired of an aged resident about the origin of the mines and road. The old man could tell only of legends and traditions, but it was presumed that the grandfathers of his compatriots were the original settlers.

Because the Old Mine Road was a major commercial thoroughfare, communities, farms, and inns rose up along it. Generations lived and died near the road. Battles were fought in its environs. Merchants, artists, soldiers, adventurers all passed along the road and played a role in its colorful history.

For the modern-day adventurer who leaves his canoe at the river's edge, a stroll along some segments of the Old Mine Road is like a trip back through time. It is easy to imagine that the environs of the Old Mine Road are little changed in over three hundred years. Fields stand in corn just as they might have long ago. There is no modern commercialism, no modern community (except the cottages), and, of course, no modern road. Some of the aged structures remain. Only the sounds of birds and the river penetrate the quiet; the smells of wild strawberry, rhododendron, fresh corn, and manure permeate the air.

There are several good places for a canoeist to explore the Old Mine Road. The first is at Mile 233.5, about one mile below Shapnack Island. This is where the summer cottages are clustered. About a mile downstream from here the road takes a very sharp left turn to a vista of a brook running through pastures and under a tiny bridge. A little further beyond, the road merges with the "Walpack Loop," a section of the Old Mine Road brought up to modern standards.

The walk upstream from Mile 233.5 is most interesting of all. The cottages are soon left behind, and the left of the road opens into extensive cornfields. In 1760 this was the farm of one John Symmes. To the right stands a magnificent stone house (now being restored by the National Park Service). This sturdy structure was built in 1742 by Isaac Van Campen. It is reputed that the last black slave in New Jersey, named Caesar, was owned by the residents of this home when slavery was abolished in New Jersey in 1829. General Horatio Gates stayed here during his service in the American Revolution, as did Congressman (later President) John Adams on his travels between Boston and Washington.

A little farther up the road, about a mile from the starting point, a giant silver maple tree stands on the right. Although its girth no doubt exceeds 15 feet and its height has been shortened by lightning or decay, the tree is nonetheless alive. Alongside this great tree is a bronze plaque and a miniature American flag, placed by the American Legion to commemorate some long-ago veteran. Behind the tree and plaque a rough trail leads steeply up into the forest. Only a hundred yards up this trail a dozen ancient tombstones are scattered on the hillside. The trees growing among the graves must be well over a hundred years old. The most prominent stone clearly marks the burial of Anna Symmes, mother-in-law of President William Henry Harrison, in 1776. Most of the other stones are very rough and illegible or unmarked.

Another good place to explore the Old Mine Road begins at Mile 230, a little below Fiddlers Elbow Rift. A short walk upstream provides a fine overlook of the rift and canoeists making their way through it. About a mile downstream on the road, to the right, a bronze plaque set in granite tells the history of the Old Mine Road. A little further is the tiny community of Flatbrookville. When Charles Hine explored the road in 1909, he commented that Flatbrookville had "a back-woods flavor that immediately appeals". Then there was a mill, an inn, and a store. Today the backwoods flavor is even more pronounced. Some of the buildings have been razed, and only a few houses and barns remain. It is a place whose time has passed.

The Old Mine Road closely approaches the river again at Mile 220, at Shoemakers Eddy by Poxono Island. This part of the road is more heavily travelled since it is the main way through the Delaware Water Gap National Recreation Area, but nevertheless rural charm prevails. A few hundred yards downstream a broad trail leads left alongside a stream called Mine Brook. Not far up this trail are the abandoned copper mines of several generations of prospectors. There is not much copper to be found here, and it is doubtful that any of the mines were ever commercially successful. The National Park Service leads tours of the mines on a regular basis in the summer. Sturdy shoes and a flashlight are advised.

On a flat area between the road and river, a bit further down, is the Old Copper Mine Inn, formerly known as Shoemaker's Union Hotel. Henry Shoemaker, a soldier of the Revolution, built a large stone house on the hillside, but this house evidently has fallen beneath the Corps of Engineers' bulldozer.

From this point all the way to the Delaware Water Gap, the road is never far from the river; though improved, it is a delight for walking and exploring and likely to reveal glimpses of its long history to the careful observer.

Indian Artifacts

Much can be told about a culture by digging through its garbage, and the garbage of aboriginal residents is abundant in the upper Delaware Valley. Recent examination of the residue of these Indians has allowed archaeologists to reconstruct the lifestyle of these early people.

It is not at all unusual for campers or canoeists to find an "arrowhead" or some other stone artifact along the banks of the Delaware. For a trained archaeologist, however, every arrowhead, or more correctly "projectile point," says something about the people who fashioned it and used it. Just as the technology and style of today's civilization differ from that of times past, so too the technology and style of Indian artifacts are indicative of the period in which they were used. By examination and correlation of many artifacts found scattered along the upper Delaware Valley and by intense excavation and study of places where Indians once lived, archaeologists have determined that several separate and distinct Indian cultures lived in the area.

When construction of the Tocks Island Dam was imminent, the Department of Interior commissioned explorations for evidence of early Indian habitation. Dr. Herbert Kraft of Seton Hall University, a frequent lecturer on the upper Delaware Valley, led the excavation of sites at Harry's Farm (in the vicinity of Tocks Island) and at the Philhower-Bell site near Minisink Island. It seems that these areas were attractive to ancient people for the same reasons that they are attractive today. At Harry's Farm, a spring provides water for people and small animals. The site is high enough above the river to be safe from floods, but near enough for good fishing and canoe access. There is plenty of firewood in the forest, and wild game—deer, waterfowl, and small animals—are abundant. Black bear and elk were once included among the game animals.

The first people in the Delaware Valley, Paleo-Indians, came soon after the last glacier retreated. Evidence of these ancient inhabitants is scant, but has been found in the form of fluted projectile points at Pahaquarry. It has been suggested that these people included the great wooly mammoth on their menu. Mammoths were no doubt present in the area at about the same time, for their remains have been found in several places in New Jersey. There seems to be, however, no direct evidence that mammoths were hunted as game.

At the Harry's Farm excavation, 90 inches below the ground surface, archaeologists have unearthed artifacts and features left by people of the valley in a period known as the Early Archaic, which occurred as long ago as 7000 B.C. Net sinkers, choppers, anvil stones, firepits and hearths, and a single projectile fragment reveal the presence of the ancient inhabitants. Sometime during the Early Archaic period the Delaware River rose in a great flood, for a layer of sand and silt a foot thick is found overlaying some of the earliest artifacts.

In the Middle Archaic period, around 3900 B.C., there appears to have been a culture distinct from earlier and later peoples. This "Kittatinny" culture is revealed in slate knives, hammer stones, milling stones, and a distinct variety of projectile points known as "Kittatinny points."

Yet another culture was present in the Delaware Valley during the late Archaic period, as long ago as 2600 B.C. These people utilized "Poplar Island" and "Lackawaxen" projectile points, which are characterized by elongated narrow blades. Abundant evidence of this culture was found at Harry's Farm site in the form of net sinkers, knives, drills, formed pebble tools, and numerous projectile points. A long transitional phase followed the Late Archaic period.

By 200 A.D. a culture known as "Woodland" had developed in the upper Delaware Valley. The Woodland period was divided into two main cultures: Early to Middle Woodland and Late Woodland. Dr. Kraft has identified two distinct cultures of the Late Woodland: the Pahaquarra and the Minisink.

Clay pottery in the form of pots, bowls, cups, and flasks was widely used in the Early to Middle Woodland culture. The changing style and decoration of pottery may be used as an index of time throughout the remaining Indian habitation. Pottery of similar characteristics was used at corresponding times over a wide geographic area, and in fact may be correlated to Indian groups in New York state, southern Canada, and the Ohio Valley.

Of all the Indians who inhabited the upper Delaware Valley, most is known of the most recent, the Late Woodland Minisink culture. These people called themselves Lenni Lenape and were known to settlers as the Delaware Indians. Indians of the Minisink disposed of their trash in refuse pits and stored their goods in lined holes in the ground. Today these pits are a bonanza for archaeologists, for they contain the remains of the everyday lives of their users. At Harry's Farm site numerous pits have been unearthed, ranging from shallow dishes to silo-shaped pits 60 inches deep. Abundant pottery sherds, occasionally an intact clay bowl or pot, food remains, tools and implements, ornaments, and other clues to Minisink life have been found.

Archaeologists working at Harry's Farm site also have discovered postmolds (the imprint and residue of wooden posts in the ground) in patterns revealing the shape and structure of Indian homes. These "long houses" were constructed by sticking saplings into the ground 2 to 3 feet apart along the edge of an oval up to 62 feet long and 22 feet wide. The saplings were bent toward the center and then joined at the top. Horizontal members were lashed along the side like a trellis, and shingles made of elm, linden, and/or chestnut bark were attached. Each long house contained a firepit, storage pits inside and nearby, and up to three rooms. At least four such houses were discovered at Harry's Farm site.

These archaeologists have been most excited by the discovery of Indian skeletons buried in shallow graves or in storage pits. Many such burials were found near Minisink Island, several at Harry's Farm site, and at least one near Dingmans Bridge. Most of the skeletons were found facing toward the west. The Lenape Indians believed, to borrow the words of Herbert Kraft, that "the sun and everything else goes toward the west, even the dead when they die," and that "the land of the spirits lies in the southwest, in the country of good hunting."

From the clues discovered by archaeologists and from the observations of the earliest pioneers and missionaries, it seems that the Indians of the upper Delaware Valley lived in family groups, not villages, about one mile apart up and down the valley. They subsisted by hunting, gathering, fishing, and gardening. They were evidently a peaceful group, for there is no evidence that their homes were fortified or built in a defensive manner. They hunted primarily with wooden bows and arrows tipped by stone points. They fished for the shad and eels that migrated, and still migrate, in the Delaware River. They gardened with crude stone hoes and cooked their meals in ornamented clay pots. The Lenape probably canoed the Delaware in hollow chestnut logs. The growing population of white settlers forced the Lenape north to Ontario and west to Ohio and Oklahoma in the early nineteenth century. Their descendents remain there to this day.

Modern canoeists and other visitors to the Delaware Valley will find collections of Indian artifacts at the High Point State Park office in New Jersey (on Route 23 at the crest of Kittatinny Ridge, four miles south of Port Jervis) and at the Pike County Historical Society Museum in Milford. Dr. Kraft and other archaeologists occasionally lecture at state and national park facilities in the area.

Finding Indian artifacts requires a sharp eye, patience, and a little luck. The best places to look are freshly eroded riverbanks and, with permission, freshly plowed fields on the flats beside the river. Locations under study by archaeologists should not be disturbed. Federal regulations prohibit removal of Indian artifacts, and any find should be reported to park service headquarters. It could be an important clue in the interpretation of early life in the Delaware Valley.

Concerts at the Watergate

A long mile up the Old Mine Road from the Depew access area a small bandshell stands at the foot of a grassy rise. On Sunday evenings each summer, the rise is speckled with little knots of people seated on blankets or prone on the grass. Strains of music fill the hollow: Bach, Bernstein, or bluegrass. This is the Watergate Recreation Area, home of weekly concerts sponsored by the National Park Service, the Artists for Environment Foundation, and the American Federation of Musicians.

When concerts began several years ago, only a few dozen listeners could be counted on the knoll. Now, as word of this free entertainment has spread, more than a thousand often gather on warm August nights. No one is disappointed. The performers that entrance so many listeners are no amateurs; they are professionals and serious students of fine arts drawn to Watergate from around the country. The concerts are of exquisite caliber consistently.

But music is only part of the performance. The bandshell is backed on the right by Watergate Pond, with children splashing at the edge and always at least one fisherman casting for an evening bass. To the left, willows flank the concert area with the Kittatinny Ridge rising steeply behind. As in all performances, timing is crucial, and at Watergate it is usually perfect: the setting sun casts a diffuse glow upon the amphitheatre, the cool stillness of evening seems to settle just at the downbeat. The orchestra seems to play only the melody—harmony is added by the laughter of children playing at the pond's edge, percussion perhaps provided by the approach of a summer storm.

In the event of rain, the concerts are held in the little church at Millbrook, about a mile further up the road. On one occasion in 1981, the audience at Watergate was impatient for the music to begin, as rain threatened to fall any moment. As the musicians entered the bandstand, the cellist announced that if rain began to fall, the concert would move. The music began, the rain poured down, and the orchestra neatly resolved at the end of about four bars—not more than 10 seconds after the downbeat. The audience burst into laughter and applause and everyone ran to their cars and the shelter of Millbrook Church.

To get to Watergate from the river—especially easy if camped at Depew Island—walk up the Depew access road to the Old Mine Road, then take a left and continue about a mile to the bandshell. Concerts start at 7:00 every Sunday evening in July and August. The National Park Service prints a schedule of performances which is available at any Delaware Water Gap National Recreation Area office or facility. Don't miss!

The Tocks Island Dam

Strictly from a canoeist's standpoint, Tocks Island is of minor interest; there are several excellent campsites found on the middle and downstream end of the island, and mild riffles gurgle on both sides. From a broader point of view, however, this sliver of land six miles upstream from the water gap is the focus of the greatest controversy ever raised concerning use of the Delaware.

In the early 1960s, after some years of study, the Delaware River Basin Commission in cooperation with the Army Corps of Engineers proposed that a great dam be built at Tocks Island to impede floodwaters. This dam would also be used to store water for consumption, provide hydroelectric power, augment low flow to prevent saltwater from moving too far upstream (to Philadelphia's freshwater intakes), and to provide recreation. This earthfill Tocks Island Dam was to be 160 feet high, stretching between the Kittatinny Ridge in New Jersey and the Pocono front in Pennsylvania. Water would be impounded in a reservoir extending 37 miles to Port Jervis.

Almost as soon as the Tocks Island proposal was announced in 1962, vocal opposition was heard from local residents (many of whom would have to leave, as their homes would be inundated) and from the budding environmental movement.

The U.S. Congress authorized the project and appropriated money for the acquisition of land that would become the bottom of the great reservoir. As acquisition proceeded, there were many ugly confrontations between the Army Corps of Engineers and local residents. In some cases, squatters moved into homes that the owners had been forced to leave. These squatters used local ser-

vices and enrolled their children in local schools, but paid no
property taxes. The government, local property owners, and
squatters all opposed each other, and conflicts intensified. Eventually the Corps of Engineers bulldozed and burned several
houses as the squatters ran into the forest, shouting oaths of vengeance. Many abandoned houses, or their foundations, remain to
this day in the area that was to be flooded.

Meanwhile, the U.S. government passed a law requiring that
an environmental impact study be made on every proposed federal project. When the environmental impact study was finally
completed for the Tocks Island Dam, it showed that the environ-
mentalists' claims had merit. The dam and reservoirs would flood
valuable natural, recreational, and historical resources. More-
over, the level of the reservoir itself would fluctuate radically,
leaving mud flats along the edges. In time, debris, silt, and vegetation would fill the reservoir. Most important for canoeists, the
reservoir also would erase 37 miles of gorgeous river travel and
replace it with a flat lake crisscrossed by motorboats.

The project lagged many years behind schedule, and projected
costs increased to many times the original estimates. The proposed dam itself had become less attractive. The Tocks Island di-
lemma had become highly visible to the public by the early 1970s.
There was political pressure—both ways—to take action on the
dam. Construction interests lobbied in Trenton and other state
capitals. A resident near Walpack on the Old Mine Road, voicing
the sentiments of many locals, posted a huge sign: "The Lord
Giveth, and the Government Taketh Away." Environmental
groups took Tocks Island as a cause célèbre and demonstrated
their views at every opportunity. The DRBC was pressed to make
a final decision.

In the summer of 1974 New Jersey Governor Brendan Byrne
announced that he would personally inspect, by canoe, the site of

the proposed dam. Many local officials, candidates, and others involved in the controversy were invited to participate. To prepare for the event, the Youth Conservation Corps (YCC) from Stokes State Forest, New Jersey, was commissioned to clean up Tocks Island itself, where the governor was to make a speech. Five dumptruck loads of garbage, including old tires and a kitchen sink, were ferried by canoe off the island.

Kittatinny Canoes donated the use of about 40 canoes for Byrne's expedition. The athletic governor took the bow seat in one, accompanied by a state trooper and a 17-year-old girl from the YCC. Then the rest of the party—dignitaries, reporters, onlookers—paddled out. At least a hundred craft were included in the flotilla as demonstrators and day paddlers joined in.

Byrne gave a short speech at Tocks Island amid a throng of demonstrators carrying signs like "Doom the Dam." He announced no decision, but said how he enjoyed the canoe trip, what a beautiful valley it was, and how his administration would study carefully the dam issue before casting its vote with the DRBC.

Over the course of the following year the governors of the four DRBC states commissioned studies, prepared reports, and conducted evaluations. But by August 1975 no final decision on Tocks Island had been reached. Governor Milton Shapp of Pennsylvania was firmly in favor of the dam. Governor Hugh Carey of New York was firmly opposed. Governor Trippett of Delaware said he would vote as New Jersey did. And New Jersey's Governor Byrne remained undecided.

Most of the responsibility in New Jersey for evaluating the dam proposal and for recommending a decision lay with David J. Bardin, Byrne's Commissioner of Environmental Protection. Bardin, of course, had studied the reports and listened to the arguments about the Tocks Island Dam. But still he was not ready to make his recommendation to the governor. Beyond the dry studies and evaluations, Bardin wanted to include his personal impressions of Tocks in the decision-making process. So he planned a visit to the scene, not as a media event but as an attempt to gain first-hand knowledge.

Accompanied only by three guides, Bardin hiked the Appalachian Trail from the water gap to Millbrook Road, a distance of 12 miles. At certain places the river could be seen clearly from the ridgetop trail, and Bardin saw hundreds of canoes making their way through the rapids and eddies. As he hiked through the afternoon, Bardin spoke with many of the other hikers he encountered. He asked them about their hometowns, about what drew them to the trail that day, and about their thoughts on the dam. Almost all the hikers knew of the Tocks Island proposal, and almost all were opposed to it.

Finally, near the trailhead at Millbrook Road, Bardin took out his pen to sign the trail register. He looked over the roster of hikers, their points of origin, and their destinations. Then, as he signed the register, Bardin commented that he would use the same pen to sign his recommendation to the governor—in opposition of the dam.

The next week the DRBC met to decide the fate of the Tocks Island Dam project. Only governor Shapp voted in favor. The dam was defeated. Since that vote in 1975, Congress has appropriated no money for the Tocks Island Dam. The project is, however, still authorized and may be pulled off the shelf if future conditions so warrant. Until then, the Delaware will remain a free-flowing river.

CAMPING AND SERVICES

Camping

All the land adjacent to the river is within the Delaware Water Gap National Recreation Area. The National Park Service has established several primitive campsites for canoeists, and unimproved camping is permitted on the river islands.

1. There are shoreline canoe campsites maintained by the National Park Service. Each has "comfort stations" but no other facilities: Hornbeck Campsite, Mile 235.1, Pennsylvania shore; Valley View Campsite, Mile 229.5, Pennsylvania shore; Walpack Bend Campsite, Mile 227.3, New Jersey shore; Hamilton Campsite, Mile 223.0, New Jersey shore.

2. Camping (one night stay only) is allowed on Shapnack Island (Mile 234.8); Buck Island (Mile 230.7 — gravel only); Depew Island (Mile 221.9); Tocks Island (Mile 217.9). On each of these islands areas have been cleared by consistent use. The ground is level, firm and without rocks, providing excellent tent sites. There are no improvements whatsoever — no outhouses, picnic tables, or firepits — so be prepared to "rough it." This section of river is very popular with canoe-campers, and the best sites are taken early.

3. The Old Copper Mine Inn (Star Route, Columbia, New Jersey 07832, 201/841 – 9550), at the site of historic Shoemakers Hotel, offers tent sites with sanitary facilities, showers, and a rec hall at River Mile 218.2.

4. Bernie's Camp-In (Dingmans Ferry, Pennsylvania 18328, 717/828 – 2266) has tent sites and sanitary facilities with showers. Located ¼ mile south of Dingmans Ferry on U.S. Route 209, River Mile 236.2.

Canoe Liveries

1. Adventure Tours (P.O. Box 631, Stroudsburg, Pennsylvania 18360, 717/223–0505) runs guided canoe tours from its base at Marshalls Creek and rents Grumman and Old Town canoes for individual use. Portage available.
2. Chamberlain Canoes (Minisink Acres, Minisink Hills, Pennsylvania 18341, 717/421–0180 rents Grumman canoes with portage from Dingmans, Bushkill, and Smithfield Beach to the water gap.
3. Kittatinny Canoes (Dingmans Ferry, Pennsylvania 18328, 717/828–2338 or 717/828–2700 operates a major canoe base at Dingmans, with portage available to most access points on the upper Delaware.

Other Services

The land adjacent to the river is publicly owned, so there are very few private services accessible.

238.5 Dingmans Ferry, Pennsylvania. Ice is available at a Texaco station .5 mile from the bridge at Dingmans.

228.2 Bushkill, Pennsylvania. Numerous motels and restaurants are located on U.S. Route 209 south of the Bushkill access area, though a walk of a mile or more may be necessary.

Tocks Island To Martins Creek

The famous Delaware Water Gap and the severe rapids at Foul Rift dominate this section, which begins as the previous section ended, with the river defining the boundary between the Appalachian Plateaus geophysical province and the Ridge and Valley Province. The Pocono Mountains are on the Pennsylvania side, and the Kittatinny Ridge is in New Jersey. At the water gap the river has gouged a 1300-foot-deep cleft in the ridge. The Delaware then flows through the Ridge and Valley Province to Manunka Chunk where it meanders through the terminal moraine of the continental glacier. Below the moraine the river falls 22 feet over the sharp limestone ledges at Foul Rift, one of the most hazardous rapids on the Delaware.

Above the water gap the river is characterized by boulder rapids separated by shallow pools. Below the gap, however, the rapids fall more severely over ledges, and the pools are much deeper. The water is 55 feet deep just below the gap; next to the pool at Narrowsburg, this is the deepest point on the river. It is 18 feet deep below Portland, 30 feet deep at Belvidere, and 42 feet deep below Foul Rift.

The Delaware Water Gap marks another change in the river. Upstream from the gap forests and little villages predominate, while below the gap the river enters more densely populated areas. The forests give way to cleared farmland, and here and there industrial centers rise from the riverbanks. There are huge cement plants at Portland, chemical refineries at Belvidere, and two giant power stations, one at Martins Creek, the other at Portland. Above the water gap the rustic Old Mine Road parallels the river on the New Jersey side. Interstate Route 80 crosses the river in the gap and runs nearby for five miles below. U.S. Route 46 continues along the New Jersey bank between Columbia and Belvidere.

The first 10 miles of this section are within the Delaware Water Gap National Recreation Area, which is part of the National Park system. The park service has several activities and exhibits accessible to canoeists. The Appalachian Trial, a continuous footpath between Georgia and Maine, crosses the Delaware River on the Interstate Route 80 bridge. There are three public access areas within the recreation area: Smithfield Beach at the head of Tocks Island, Worthington State Forest at Mile 214.7, and Kittatinny Point access in the water gap. Below the water gap private access sites are maintained by electric utility companies and are open for use by the public during daylight.

RIVER GUIDE

217.1. Downstream end of Tocks Island. This is the site of the proposed Tocks Island Dam. (See the features section of the preceding chapter.) A slight riffle runs from the channels on both sides of the island.

217.0. Pass under high-tension line, with a clear cut through the forest on the New Jersey side.

216.8. Two small islands are nestled against the Pennsylvania shore.

216.7. Upstream end of Labar Island. Channels to the left and right are passable without obstructions.

216.1. Downstream end of Labar Island. Upstream end of

PA

Tocks Is.

218

217

SHAWNEE
ON DELAWARE

(A)

Woodcock Bar

Labar Is.

216

(L)

(F)

Depue Is.

215

Shawnee Pt.

Muskrat Is.

Access

NJ

(C)

Shawnee Is.

214

Brodhead Cr.

Worthington State
Forest

[I]

213

Schellenbergers Is.

[I]

Gap Iss.

Dunnfield Cr.

Water Gap

211

Access

212

DELAWARE
WATER GAP

[I]

Arrow Is.

[I]

(C)

210

(H)

Slateford Cr.

KEY

▲ Camping

(C) Canoe Livery

(F) Food

(L) Lodging

(H) Historic Site

(A) Arts

[I] White Water
Classification

Woodcock Bar, a slender island extending diagonally downstream. The main channel is on the left, with shallows and exposed gravel bars. The channel to the right is passable, though at low water the entrance to it is nearly blocked by gravel bars.

215.9. Upstream end of Depue Island, in the right channel behind Woodcock Bar. Depue Island extends one mile downstream against the Pennsylvania shore. The main channel is to the left, but the narrow right channel is passable. Worthington State Forest Campground is on the New Jersey shore.

214.7. Downstream end of Depue Island.

214.6. Worthington State Forest access area, New Jersey side, with paved boat ramp, sanitary facilities, trash disposal, telephones, and fresh water. The forest office is a few feet from the boat ramp.

Shawnee Point, between Depue Island upstream and Shawnee Island downstream, is on the Pennsylvania shore opposite the Worthington access. The Shawnee Inn, white with a red roof, stands near the point. The Shawnee is the last of the great resort hotels on the Delaware River. Vacation havens at the Delaware Water Gap and at Shohola disappeared decades ago, but the Shawnee Inn has kept up with the times. Developed by C. C. Worthington in 1910 as the Buckwood Inn, the Shawnee became known as one of the finest golf resorts in the country. In the 1940s the property was taken over by Fred Waring, the musical Pennsylvanian. The Shawnee Inn today is a complete resort community, with the 100-room inn, private cottages, time-shared condominiums, swimming, nightclub entertainment, and the Delaware River. The famous Shawnee Playhouse is nearby in the community of Shawnee-on-Delaware.

Upstream end of Muskrat Island on the left side of the river. Channel to the left is clear. There is a moderate current in the main channel on the right.

Upstream end of Shawnee Island, which extends 1.2 miles along the Pennsylvania shore. The main flow of the river is between the New Jersey shore and the island, but the narrow channel between Shawnee Island and the Pennsylvania shore is passable. The second and seventeenth holes of the famous Shawnee Resort Golf Course cross the channel shortly after its entrance. The channel bottom is usually littered with hundreds of golf balls which can be scooped up by canoers. Golf balls carried by the current are often seen on the river bottom well below the water gap.

213.4. Downstream end of Shawnee Island.

213.2. Pass under high-tension line.

213.1. The New Jersey abutment and two piers remain from the old Lackawanna Railroad Bridge, which washed away in 1955.

Brodhead Creek enters, Pennsylvania side. The creek has built gravel bars that extend two-thirds of the way across the river.

Ledges on the New Jersey side are covered with graffiti.

Upstream end of Schellenbergers Island. The Pennsylvania channel is dry at moderate water level, although a branch of Brodhead Creek enters the channel slightly downstream.

213.0. A Class I rapid with standing waves to 1½ feet near the New Jersey shore.

212.5. Gap Islands on the right side of the river. Channels on the right are passable at moderate water level. A Class I rapid is in the main channel near the New Jersey shore with standing waves to 1½ feet and no obstructions.

212.2. Pass under the Delaware Water Gap Toll Bridge, completed in 1953 and carrying Interstate Route 80. The Appalachian Trail, extending from Georgia to Maine, crosses this bridge. (See the features section of this chapter.)

212.1. The river bends sharply left, entering the famous Delaware Water Gap. (See description in the features section of this chapter.) Hemlock woods cover the steep Pennsylvania slopes on the right.

211.7. Kittatinny access area on the New Jersey side. A broad sand beach with a corduroy boat ramp. This is one of the busiest access areas anywhere on the river. The Kittatinny Point Visitor Center of the Delaware Water Gap National Recreation Area is at the top of the bluff above the beach. There are rest rooms, fresh water, and shaded picnic tables. Information about activities in the recreation area is available here. (For further details, see the features section of this chapter.)

211.5. Dunnfield Creek enters, New Jersey side. The rock profile of an Indian, with forest headdress, can be seen on the New Jersey cliffs ahead.

211.0. Steep cliffs and landslides on both sides.

210.8. Upstream end of Arrow Island. The New Jersey channel is narrow and begins and ends with a Class I rapid. At low water the Pennsylvania channel is nearly blocked by shallows. The main current flows near the New Jersey shore in moderate standing waves.

210.6. Downstream end of Arrow Island. Rocky ledges extend from Pennsylvania shore. There are numerous protruding and barely submerged boulders on the left for the next .2 mile.

210.1. A small stream enters, New Jersey side.

209.5. Slateford Creek enters, Pennsylvania side. A small gravel bar extends into river.

209.0. Stony Brook enters, New Jersey side, with a gravel bar extending .1 mile downstream. Current increases over boulders and shallows to a Class I rapid, then passes under the compound arches of the Erie-Lackawanna Railroad Bridge. Immediately under the bridge a Class I+ rapid flows from left to right with a few boulders. Standing waves to 2 feet continue downstream .1 mile.

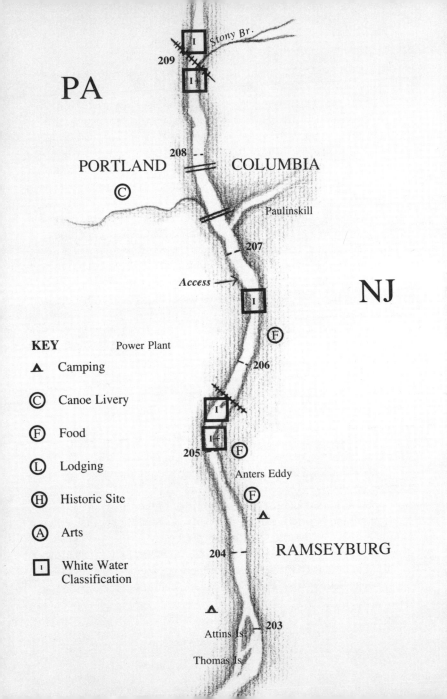

PA

Stony Br.

209

PORTLAND   208   COLUMBIA

Ⓒ

Paulinskill

207

Access →

NJ

Ⓕ

206

KEY   Power Plant
▲ Camping

Ⓒ Canoe Livery

Ⓕ Food

Ⓛ Lodging

Ⓗ Historic Site

Ⓐ Arts

[I] White Water
    Classification

205

Ⓕ

Anters Eddy

Ⓕ

▲

204   RAMSEYBURG

▲

Attins Is.   203

Thomas Is.

207.6. Pass under the Portland-Columbia Pedestrian Bridge. The last wooden covered bridge to span the Delaware was washed from these piers in the flood of August 1955. The original bridge was built in 1839. The present four-span steel bridge was completed in 1958 on the original piers and abutments and is open only to pedestrians. The original bridge house stands just upstream.

207.3. Pass under the Portland-Columbia Toll Bridge, opened to traffic in 1953. This bridge was constructed to replace the aging covered bridge upstream. A moderate riffle begins under the bridge. The communities of Columbia, New Jersey, and Portland, Pennsylvania, stand at opposite ends of the bridge. Limestone quarried in the vicinity is used in the manufacture of Portland cement.

207.1. The Paulinskill River enters, New Jersey side.

206.7. Metropolitan Edison access area, maintained by the Metropolitan Edison Electric Company, provides a dirt ramp, limited parking, trash disposal, sanitary facilities, and a few picnic tables. The access gate is locked at night.

206.4. A Class I rapid with a few protruding boulders.

206.3. Pass under high tension lines.

206.2. The Metropolitan Edison Electric Generating Plant, with two high smokestacks, stands on the Pennsylvania shore. A concrete cooling water outfall extends into the middle of the river—stay clear.

205.4. Pass under the five-span bridge of the Delaware, Lackawanna, and Western Railroad. There is a small gravel island on the left side of the river just below the bridge.

205.3. A Class I rapid with standing waves to 1½ feet flows along the Pennsylvania shore. The left three-quarters of the river is very shallow. Eagles Nest, a private camp, is on the New Jersey bank.

205.2. Rapids increase in severity (to Class I +) along the Pennsylvania shore. Be wary of a few just submerged boulders.

204.9. Enters Anters Eddy, continuing 2.5 miles downstream.

204.0. The little community of Ramseyburg, New Jersey, is on the left.

203.2. Upstream end of Attins Island, with the main channel to the left.

202.9. Downstream end of Attins Island; upstream end of Thomas Island. Main channel continues on the left, but the passage between the islands is navigable. Thomas Island continues .2 mile downstream.

202.4. Upstream end of Dildine Island. The main channel is to the right and begins with a Class I rapid. The left channel is also passable and opens into a maze of small islands, gravel bars, and winding passages. There are Class I rapids in some of these small channels.

201.4. Downstream end of Dildine Island. A Class I rapid flows at the end of the Pennsylvania channel. Dildine Island is privately owned, and there are a few cottages with boat landings.

201.0. River bends sharply right. This is the vicinity of the terminal moraine of the great Wisconsin ice sheet, the last continental glacier in North America. Fifteen thousand years ago the area north of this point was buried under one mile of ice. The terminal moraine itself is an undulating mound of rocks extending from Staten Island, across New Jersey, through Pennsylvania, and into Ohio and the Midwest.

Huffman-LaRoche Chemical Plant is on the New Jersey shore.

200.6. Upstream end of Macks Island. Long Rift, a Class I rapid, flows between the island and the Pennsylvania bank. The rift begins with a series of waves, then falls over a small rocky ledge 100 yards downstream from the head of the island. There is a second ledge near the downstream end of the island. The left

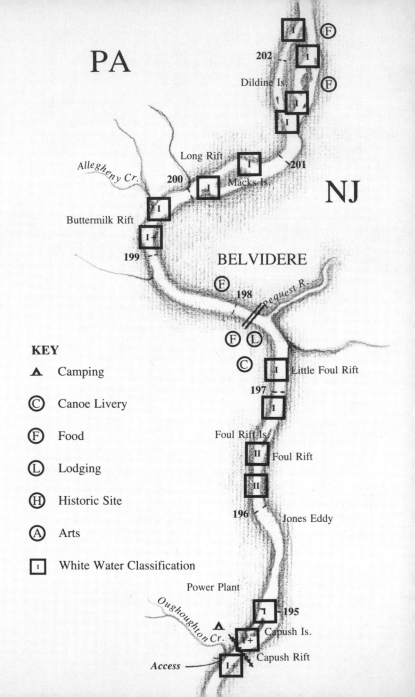

PA

Allegheny Cr.

Long Rift

200

Buttermilk Rift

199

202

Dildine Is.

201

Macks Is.

NJ

BELVIDERE

F

198

Pequest R.

F L

C

Little Foul Rift

197

Foul Rift Is.

II Foul Rift

II

196 Jones Eddy

KEY

▲ Camping

Ⓒ Canoe Livery

Ⓕ Food

Ⓛ Lodging

Ⓗ Historic Site

Ⓐ Arts

[I] White Water Classification

Power Plant

Oughoughton Cr.

I 195

I+ Capush Is.

Access I+ Capush Rift

channel is passable but shallow at low water level. There is a stony ledge where the left channel rejoins the main channel at the downstream end of the island.

200.0. Small stream enters, Pennsylvania side.

199.8. A small road approaches the river very closely on the Pennsylvania side. This is the site of Hartzell's Ferry, discontinued around the turn of the century.

199.6. Allegheny Creek enters, Pennsylvania side, with a gravel bar constricting the river by nearly one-half. Enter Buttermilk Rift, a Class I+ rapid. The main channel flows from the New Jersey shore to the center of the river. Near the Pennsylvania bank the channel is peppered with submerged and protruding boulders that require skillful maneuvering.

199.3. The second ledge of Buttermilk Rift. Watch for submerged rocks on the left.

199.1. The third and final ledge of Buttermilk Rift. The main channel is in the middle with standing waves to 2 feet. Submerged ledges extend from both banks.

198.7. Small stream enters, Pennsylvania side.

197.8. Pass under Riverton-Belvidere Bridge. The abutments and piers were constructed in 1836 to support a wooden bridge. The present four-span steel structure was built in 1904 after the old bridge was washed down in the flood of 1903. The community of Belvidere, New Jersey, county seat of Warren County, is at the east end of the bridge. The Pequest River enters immediately downstream from the bridge, New Jersey side.

197.4. A small stream enters, New Jersey side.

197.3. Enter Little Foul Rift, a Class I rapid. Shallows on the left and rock ledges on the right may be hazardous at low water. Main channel is through the center.

196.7. Enter Foul Rift, beginning as Class I but building quickly to a Class II rapid. The river drops 22 feet in the next .5

mile. This is among the most severe rapids on the Delaware and should be avoided by beginners. There is no developed portage around the rapid, but at moderate water level canoeists can beach on a gravel bar on the New Jersey bank and carry their canoes along the bars and ledges to calmer water. Foul Rift begins with a cluster of angular boulders in the center of the river. There are passages left and right of center, but here too submerged and protruding rocks are a hazard.

196.6. Upstream end of Foul Rift Island, an exposed rock ledge parallel to the Pennsylvania shore. The narrow channel to the right of the island is passable with few obstructions and is the safest route. The main channel left of the island is peppered with boulders and ledges.

196.5. Downstream end of Foul Rift Island. Exposed ledges begin extending from the New Jersey shore. Current flows left to right. Rapids become much more severe with many submerged and protruding boulders. The safest passage remains ner the Pennsylvania shore.

196.3. The final ledge of Foul Rift, extending entirely across the river with a sudden drop of about 3 feet. At low water parts of the ledge are exposed, with a gap and high standing waves in the center. The channel near the Pennsylvania shore is also passable. This ledge was one of the most severe hazards to timber rafts.

196.1. Numerous rock ledges and islands extend from the New Jersey shore for the next .2 mile. Clearest channel is along the Pennsylvania shore.

196.0. Enter Jones Eddy. Timber raftsmen pulled up here to collect their composure and equipment after running Foul Rift. Modern canoeists can do likewise.

195.5. The coal-fired Metropolitan Edison Power Plant is on the Pennsylvania shore. The twin giant cooling towers are landmarks for miles around.

194.9. Upstream end of Capush Island. The channel along the Pennsylvania shore is impassable at low water. Capush Rift, starting as Class I but building quickly to a Class I+ rapid, begins in the main channel left of the island. There is a broad gravel bar in the center of the channel. Just below this bar the river falls over a rock ledge; protruding and submerged rocks may be a hazard at low water. The best channel is in the middle with standing waves to 1½ feet.

194.4. Capush Rift continues, falling over another ledge with shallows on the right. Best passage is in the left center of the river. Gravel bars on the right may be exposed at low water level.

194.3. Pass under Penn Central Railroad siding. Capush Rift ends under the bridge with standing waves to 2 feet in the middle and left of river.

194.2. Martins Creek access area, Pennsylvania side. This facility is owned and maintained by the Pennsylvania Power and Light Company and offers limited parking, trash disposal, a wide gravel ramp, and camping by permit. Oughoughton Creek enters at the gravel ramp and must be crossed to reach the access. Canoeists should plan to do some wading when using this access. A gate to the area is locked at night.

FEATURES

Delaware Water Gap National Recreation Area

The Delaware Water Gap National Recreation Area (DWGNRA) was planned originally as a complement to the Tocks Island Lake. It was expected that more than 10 million people a year would visit the park, primarily for lake-oriented recreation. Of course, the Tocks Island Dam was never built and, evidently, will not be for a long time, if ever. Beginning in 1966 the federal government acquired most of the land for the would-be lake bottom as well as additional lands along the river for recreational use. Seventy thousand acres will be included eventually in the recreation area, which will be joined to Worthington and Stokes State Forests and High Point State Park. Almost all of the northwestern edge of New Jersey will be publicly owned for recreational use. With the demise of the dam and with the realization that local roads and services could not meet the demands of 10 million visitors a year, the National Park Service developed more modest plans for the administration and use of the recreation area. Low intensity recreation, such as hiking, nature study, hunting, fishing, and of course canoeing, is now regarded as the best use of the recreation area.

The population within the area encompassed by DWGNRA, especially the New Jersey portions, was never very great. Pahaquarry Township, which covers about 50 square miles, could claim only 50 residents in 1970. When lands were acquired by the government for the lake and park, many of the residents had to leave, some of them against their will. Throughout the recreation area, especially along the Old Mine Road in New Jersey, the foundations of many abandoned and razed homes can be seen in the forest. The fertile lands along the river have always been excellent for a variety of crops, and considerable acreage within the park is used for farming under a permit system. Extensive cornfields can be seen from the river and along many of the roads within the park.

The National Park Service conducts and sponsors a great variety of activities and exhibits within the recreation area. Some of these are within walking distance of the river, while others may be taken in on the way to or from a canoe trip. Of particular interest to beginners are the canoe trips led by the National Park Service from the Smithfield Beach and Bushkill access areas. A guide teaches basic canoeing skills and water safety and discusses the natural and human history of the area. The park service does not provide canoes.

Cultural History. The National Park Service has a number of programs and exhibits devoted to interpreting the human history of the area. At the Slateford Farm, about one-half mile off Pennsylvania route 611 (approximately Mile 209.5 on the river), a middle-class farmhouse of the 1800s has been reconstructed. Costumed interpreters conduct tours of the house and demonstrate nineteenth-century farming techniques. An abandoned slate quarry is in the vicinity and may be visited on a guided nature walk that begins near the farm.

Millbrook Village, a partially reconstructed community of the eighteenth and nineteenth centuries, is found two miles north of the Depew access area on the Old Mine Road. The little village includes a blacksmith shop, general store, gristmill, church, school, and several historic homes. Reconstructed and used as they were 150 years ago, these buildings provide unusual insight into an American way of life long vanished. Millbrook had about 75 residents in the mid-1800s, but the little crossroads community dwindled as commerce concentrated in the cities. Until the park service acquired the lands in the 1970s, Millbrook remained a backwater of American history.

The historic Old Mine Road and Indian artifacts found within the DWGNRA are discussed in more detail in the features section of the preceding chapter.

An Environment for Art. The Delaware Water Gap has always been a favorite of artists, a tradition carried on in several programs sponsored by the National Park Service. At the village of Walpack Center, seven miles south of U.S. Route 206 on New Jersey Route 521, the Artists for Environment Foundation maintains its headquarters. Artists for Environment is sponsored by the National Park Service and is affiliated with the Union of Independent Colleges of Art. Students and professionals come here every year to practice their crafts. The foundation has set up also the Water Gap Art Gallery one-half mile south of Walpack Center. Here on exhibit are the works of well-known professional artists and a permanent collection of works portraying the natural and cultural heritage of the water gap region.

The entire community of Peters Valley, 2½ miles north of Walpack Center, is a living art studio. Woodwork, pottery, textiles, and metal sculpture are taught and practiced in what were once homes and barns. The studios themselves are closed to the public, but an information center and craft store are available to visitors. The Peters Valley crafts fair is held the last weekend of every July. Exhibits, demonstrations, and sales are clustered in a hayfield just up the hill from Peters Valley. This event attracts a great number of visitors every year. A visit to the crafts fair is a good way to begin or end a canoe trip.

Concerts at the Watergate Recreation Center are discussed in the features section of the preceding chapter.

Environmental Education. There are three centers for formal environmental education within the DWGNRA. These may be found at Thunder Mountain and Walpack Valley in New Jersey and at the Pocono Environmental Education Center four miles south of Dingmans Ferry on U.S. Route 209 in Pennsylvania (about Mile 234 on the river). Pocono Center was originally a honeymoon resort, but it is now used for classes and seminars in environmental studies. Programs are conducted by the faculty of nearby Keystone Junior College. A trail for the blind has been developed at the Pocono Center, and visitors may use this trail to discover their perceptions of nature without using their eyes.

Interpretive nature walks are guided by park service experts at the Slateford Farm, Dingmans Falls, and Smithfield Beach. At Point of Gap, on the Pennsylvania bank at River Mile 211, an exhibit illustrates the geology of the water gap.

Information about current activities within the DWGNRA can be found at most of the National Park Service facilities. The Kittatinny Point information station, located at the Kittatinny access area (River Mile 211.7, New Jersey side), is easily accessible from the river and from Interstate Route 80. Park service personnel are on hand to assist visitors—including canoeists—in enjoying the recreation area.

Delaware Water Gap

The Delaware Water Gap is the single most famous and spectacular natural feature along the Delaware River. Here the river has cut through the hard solid rock of the Kittatinny Ridge to form a cleft 1300 feet deep, 1500 yards across at the top and 300 yards across at the bottom. Kittatinny Mountain is a "ridge" of the Ridge and Valley geophysical province: a single, folded mountain extending from New York state, where it is known as the Shawangunk, through New Jersey, into Pennsylvania (where the ridge is known as Blue Mountain), and south into Maryland and Virginia. Numerous other rivers cut through the ridge, including the Lehigh, Susquehanna, and Potomac.

The geologic formations of the water gap are well known. Hundreds of millions of years ago, during the Silurian period, the continents of Europe and North America were not separated. Great rivers flowed westward from ancient high mountains in Europe. Pebbles and sand were eroded from the mountains, carried off by rivers, and deposited over what is now eastern North America. As the mountains were eroded further and the sea level rose, the sediment became finer and finer until only sand, silt, and the debris of

View south from the Delaware Water Gap. Arrow Island, with Class I rapids on either side, is seen in the distance. Photo by the author.

marine animals were deposited. These layers of sediment, thousands of feet thick, were compressed and solidified into rock. As the continents separated, intense pressure caused the layers of rock to heave and fold, creating new mountains. The remnants of these mountains exist today as the Ridge and Valley Province, including the Kittatinny Ridge. The layers of rock can be seen clearly at the Delaware Water Gap. The rocks tilt generally to the northwest, with the oldest rocks on the bottom.

Moving downstream through the water gap, the canoeist first encounters the red and green sandstones of the High Falls Formation (known in Pennsylvania as the Bloomsburg Formation). Indeed the river parallels the strike of this layer of rock for several miles above the water gap. In the middle of the gap the sandstone grades into a pebbly, gray-white conglomerate called the Shawangunk Formation. These are the sediments that rivers carried off from ancient European mountains to form the southeastern front of the Kittatinny Ridge. The layering of this rock can be seen clearly above landslides on both the Pennsylvania and New Jersey sides. A close inspection reveals intricate crossbedding caused by minor currents in the ancient rivers. Here and there in the Shawangunk Formation geologists have found very thin layers of shale that were formed by the deposition of silt and mud in eddies of the ancient rivers. Fossils of extinct lobsterlike creatures called eurypterids have been discovered in these black deposits.

How the water gap itself was created is not certain. The Delaware River is deflected by the Kittatinny Ridge at Port Jervis and runs parallel to the ridge until the river breaks through it at the gap. It is likely that the river once flowed on a plane much higher than at present, above the present-day Kittatinny Ridge. As the river eroded overlying layers of rock, it maintained its approximate course by cutting through a weak point in the Shawangunk conglomerate formation. Over eons this weak point was eroded deeper and deeper and eventually became the Delaware Water Gap. Glaciers in recent geologic history rounded and shaped the gap into its present form. The water gap is still being eroded, as evidenced by the great landslides on both sides.

The water gap was an early mecca for vacationers. In 1833 a small hotel called Kittatinny House opened under the Pennsylvania cliffs at the water gap. In later decades of the nineteenth century the water gap became even more popular with tourists and artists. By 1877 the Kittatinny House was five stories high and had hundreds of rooms. Several other Victorian-style hotels, including the great Water Gap House, were built on the Pennsylvania banks. The hotels, however, eventually suffered by their own intense rivalry and by improved transportation, which made other tourist havens more accessible. One by one the grand old hotels disappeared, until the Kittatinny House itself burned to the ground in 1931. Today only its foundation remains.

The Appalachian Trail

White rectangles, precisely 2½ inches wide by 6 inches tall, are painted at intervals along the walkway on the I-80 bridge at the Delaware Water Gap. From the Pennsylvania end of the bridge, these blazes lead into the woods and may be followed all the way to Springer Mountain, Georgia. From the New Jersey end the marks follow along Dunnfield Creek and eventually lead to Mt. Katahdin in Maine. The white blazes identify the Appalachian Trail, a footpath that extends 2,015 miles along the ridge tops of the Appalachian Mountains.

The Appalachian Trail is not, as some think, an old Indian trail. The Indians for the most part stayed in the valleys. Rather, the trail can be credited primarily to one man, Benton MacKaye, who conceived of the trail at the turn of the century and had the vision and perseverance to make it a reality.

The first section of the Appalachian Trail was marked and cleared in 1923 near Bear Mountain, New York. In 1937 the Civilian Conservation Corps axed the last portions of the trail through the swamps of Maine. The corridor of the Appalachian Trail is now protected by federal law, and in New Jersey all of the trail is on public land.

Until 1970 only a handful of people had actually hiked the entire trail from Georgia to Maine. But with the increased popularity of outdoor recreation, the number of "end-to-enders" has mushroomed. Now, more than a hundred hikers every year can claim rightly the coveted "Georgia to Maine" patch for their backpacks. Most people who hike the entire Appalachian Trail start in Georgia in early spring, then work their way north with the season, arriving in Maine in September or October, just as snow begins to fall. To keep to this timetable the long-distance hikers must cross the Delaware in June or July.

End-to-end hikers are easy to spot. Unlike many day hikers, they don't seem to be in a hurry yet they cover a lot of ground fast. Their shirts are worn to glossy smoothness at the shoulder. Their backpacks are a study in economy. Their boots are well oiled and in excellent repair, better than new. Every end-to-ender has his own personal reason for being on the trail. A man of about 60 explained that one day his wife left him; the next day he started walking the trail. He had never hiked before and said he never would again. He reshouldered his pack, tapped the tobacco in his pipe, and vanished alone into the forest toward Maine.

At the Delaware Water Gap the Appalachian Trial is easily accessible to canoeists. In New Jersey the trail leads from the DWGNRA Information Center under I-80 and through a dark hemlock ravine along cascading Dunnfield Creek. In about three miles the trail reaches Sunfish Pond, a crystal-clear lake carved by the glacier at the top of Kittatinny Ridge. This particular segment of the Appalachian Trail is among the most popular, and there are almost always a considerable number of hikers. The traffic has worn and eroded the footway, and much of the trail to Sunfish Pond is rough walking as a result. Unfortunately, too, unconcerned and inconsiderate hikers leave their litter behind them, making the trail less pleasant for others. National Park and State Park personnel, along with volunteers, police the area well, and there are frequent arrests for illegal camping and littering. A roundtrip hike to Sunfish Pond on the Appalachian Trail takes about five hours.

In Pennsylvania the Appalachian Trail leads steeply to the summit of Mt. Minsi (elevation 1463 feet). This trail is somewhat less popular but affords outstanding overlooks of the Delaware Water Gap. It is about two miles—a roundtrip of three hours—to the summit.

An interesting, fairly easy side trail leads off the Appalachian Trail in New Jersey to the summit of Mt. Tammany (elevation 1527 feet). This trail, marked by blue blazes, arrives at the summit after 2.5 miles for a panoramic view of the water gap and the river to the south. Hikers may return on the trail blazed with red dots to the rest area along I-80, a short distance east of the Kittatinny Information Center.

CAMPING AND SERVICES

Camping

1. Camping is permitted for one night only on Tocks Island and Labar Island. Sites have been cleared by consistent use. There are no facilities or maintenance, so be prepared to rough it.

2. Worthington State Forest (Worthington State Forest, Old Mine Road, Columbia, New Jersey 07832, 201/841–9575) has about 80 campsites on the river's edge between Mile 216 and Mile 214. Each site has a picnic table and fireplace, with drinking water nearby. It must be noted that Worthington State Park is very popular with "car campers," and it is often difficult to find an available site on weekends.

3. The Delaware River Campgrounds (Located between the

river and New Jersey Route 46 at Mile 204.1, New Jersey, 201/475–4517) offers tent sites.

4. Driftstone on the Delaware (River Road, R.D. 1, Mt. Bethel, Pennsylvania 18343, 717/897–6859) is a full-service campground offering tent sites, showers, laundry, a rec hall, and a camp store. It is located at Mile 203.4 with direct access from the river.
5. Foxwood Farm Family Campground (Box 431A, R.D. 1, East Stroudsburg, Pennsylvania 18301, 717/421–1424) is a campground resort primarily oriented to recreational vehicle camping. There are tent sites, however, and complete facilities, including showers, a rec hall, a swimming pool and a camp store. Foxwood Farm is accessible from the river near Shawnee Island at Mile 214.5.

Canoe Liveries

1. Shawnee Canoe Trips (P.O. Box 147, Marshalls Creek, Pennsylvania 18335, 717/223–0770) rents Grumman and Blue Hole canoes for individuals or groups. Shawnee specializes in trips through the water gap, Walpack Bend, and Foul Rift and is located on U.S. Route 209, 3.6 miles north of I-80. Reservations are encouraged.
2. Northland Canoe Outfitters (Marshalls Creek, Pennsylvania 18335, 717/223–0275) is located on U.S. Route 209, 3 miles north of I-80. Northland will provide portage for a fee.
3. Adventure Tours (P.O. Box 175, Marshalls Creek, Pennsylvania 18335, 717/223–0505) specializes in completely outfitted and guided canoe expeditions. The weekend excursion starts upstream from the water gap and includes some of the white water below. Canoes, camping equip-

ment, and all meals are provided. This is an excellent program for beginners or for groups who want a very relaxing
weekend. Reservations are necessary. Adventure Tours also
rents Grumman and Old Town canoes for individual use and
will provide portage. Adventure Tours is located on U.S.
Route 209, 2 miles north of I-80.

4. Chamberlain Canoes (Minisink Acres, Minisink Hills,
   Pennsylvania 18341, 717/421–0180) runs trips from
   Smithfield Beach, Bushkill, or Dingmans Ferry to its home
   base, Grumman canoes are provided. Reservations have
   first priority with transportation. Chamberlain Canoes is located on River Road one mile north of I-80 (Exit 53).

5. Water Gap Canoes (P.O. Box 213, Delaware Water Gap,
   Pennsylvania 18327, 717/476–0398) rents Coleman and
   Grumman canoes, with portage, for "canoe trips from three
   hours to four days." Water Gap Canoes has groceries, ice,
   bait, and tents available. Located on Pennsylvania Route
   611, ¾ mile from I-80 (Exit 53).

6. Doe Hollow Canoe Rentals (R.D. 2, Department BR,
   Bangor, Pennsylvania 18013, 215/498–5103 ext. 666)
   rents canoes and other river craft by the hour or day. Portage is available to any access area. Doe Hollow is located
   one road mile from the river in Riverton, Pennsylvania,
   across from Belvidere, New Jersey.

7. Pack Shack Adventures (Delaware Water Gap, Pennsylvania 18327, 717/424–8533) has canoes, kayaks, and camping gear for rent. Though this outfitter is not on the river,
   trips can be arranged on the Delaware between Port Jervis
   and Martins Creek.

8. Port and Land Sport Shop (Portland, Pennsyslvania,
   717/897–5244) has canoes and equipment for rent.

Other Services

There are no commercial services accessible from the river within the Delaware Water Gap National Recreation Area, Worthington State Forest, or on Interstate Route 80 in New Jersey.

206.0 South of Columbia, New Jersey. The Log Cabin Inn, a small tavern featuring pizza, on U. S. Route 46 adjacent to river.

204.4 Ramseyburg, New Jersey. Hunters Lodge Restaurant and Motel.

204.3 Ramscyburg, New Jersey The Delaware Truck Stop and Diner, and the Humpty Dumpty Ice Cream and Snack Bar, on U.S. Route 46, may be reached via a dirt road leading from a high sandy bluff, just downstream from Eagle Nest Camp.

204.2 Ramseyburg, New Jersey. Buckwood Inn.

203.8 Ramseyburg, New Jersey. Marshall's Farm Market operates during the summer and early fall 100 yards from the river.

202.3 New Jersey. Washburn's Wildwood Food and Bar, on U.S. Route 46.

202.0 New Jersey. King Cole Grove, on U.S. Route 46, has a number of picnic tables on the riverbanks and features ice cream and chili dogs at its snack bar.

197.8 Riverton, Pennsylvania. Riverton Hotel and Restaurant is at the Pennsylvania end of the Belvidere Bridge.

197.8 Belvidere, New Jersey. Contains a supermarket, pharmacy, movie theatre, and several restaurants.

Martins Creek to Upper Black Eddy

This section is nearly 28 miles long. Considerable perseverance is required to canoe the entire length in one day, and even the hardiest paddlers will be bone-tired when finished.

The river continues to flow through the Ridge and Valley geophysical province and cuts through several small water gaps. Bedrock is exposed in many places, and ledges create numerous moderate rapids. Between rapids the pools are moderately deep, up to 35 feet below Raubsville. Just below Rieglesville the river leaves the Ridge and Valley and enters the Piedmont geophysical province, a broad band of rolling hardrock hills extending between New Jersey and northern Georgia. Between Rieglesville and Upper Black Eddy are found the 500-foot-high red sandstone Palisades of the Delaware that are characteristic of the Piedmont. The Lehigh River, one of the Delaware's major tributaries, enters the river at the Forks of the Delaware at Easton, Pennsylvania.

Farmland continues to dominate the countryside along the river, with the exception of the twin cities of Phillipsburg, New Jersey, and Easton, Pennsylvania. U.S. Route 611 parallels the river on the Pennsylvania side between Martins Creek and Rieglesville. Below Rieglesville, Pennsylvania, Route 32 runs nearby. There are 12 access areas in this section, 6 clustered at Easton and Phillipsburg. The others are located at Martins Creek at the beginning of this section, Sandts Eddy at Mile 189.9, Frys Run Park at Mile 176. 7, Rieglesville at Mile 174.6, Holland Church at Mile 173.7, and Upper Black Eddy at this section's end.

The Delaware Canal, the last operating towpath canal in America, parallels the river on the Pennsylvania side below Easton. Canoeists can make use of the canal for circle trips. After travelling downstream, canoeists can portage to the canal and return to the starting point upstream.

RIVER GUIDE

194.2. Martins Creek access area, owned and maintained by the Pennsylvania Power and Light Company. A wide gravel ramp leads to the river at the mouth of Oughoughton Creek. Limited parking, trash disposal, and camping by permit. The gate to the access area is closed at night.

193.4. A Class I rapid in a river "narrows." No major obstructions.

192.2. Buckhorn Creek enters, New Jersey side. River turns sharply right.

191.6. Keifer Island begins in the middle of the river. Smalleys Rift, a Class I rapid, begins in both left and right channels at the upstream end of the island. Standing waves to 1½ feet.

191.3. Keifer Island ends. Right channel turns sharply left to rejoin mainstream in a gravelly riffle. Smalleys Rift, a Class I rapid, continues in the left channel and mainstream, with a few boulders in right center.

191.2. Extensive gravel mining operations, New Jersey side.

190.7. Pass under railroad bridge. Martins Creek enters, Pennsylvania side, immediately downstream from the bridge. Smokestacks of Martins Creek Cement Plant are visible on the Pennsylvania shore. Community of Martins Creek Station on New Jersey shore.

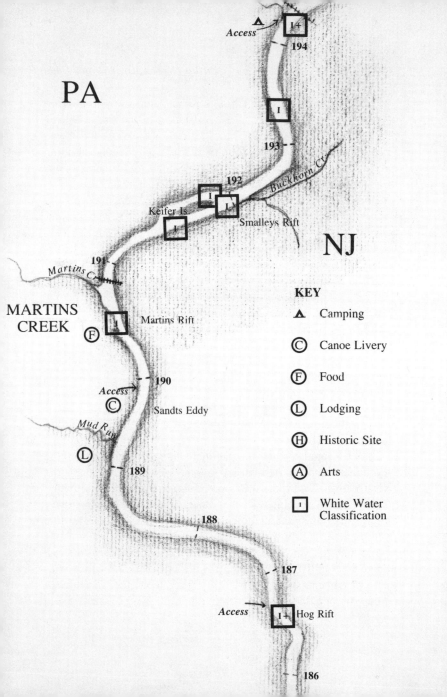

PA

194

I

193

Buckhorn Cr.

192

I

Keifer Is.

L

I

Smalleys Rift

NJ

Martins Cr.

191

MARTINS
CREEK

F

I   *Martins Rift*

190

Access

C

Sandts Eddy

Mud Run

L

189

188

187

Access   I+   Hog Rift

186

Access   ▲   I+

KEY

▲   Camping

Ⓒ   Canoe Livery

Ⓕ   Food

Ⓛ   Lodging

Ⓗ   Historic Site

Ⓐ   Arts

☐I   White Water
Classification

190.4. Martins Rift, a Class I rapid, with current moving slightly from right to left, in a constriction of the river. Gravel bars on New Jersey side.

189.9. A moderate riffle, then river slows into Sandts Eddy for next 2 miles. There are numerous powerboats and waterskiers in this section; canoeists should stay near either shore.

Sandts Eddy access area, Pennsylvania side, operated by the Pennsylvania Fish Commission. A boat ramp to the river, limited parking, trash disposal, sanitary facilities, and picnic area.

Moderate riffle marks the end of Sandts Eddy. River bends widely left.

189.2. Mud Run enters, Pennsylvania side.

187.2. Another moderate riffle. Numerous boat docks along New Jersey shore. River bends sharply to the right.

186.5. Frost Hollow Park access area, Pennsylvania side. Maintained by the North Hampton County Division of Parks and Recreation. Includes a boat ramp, limited parking, picnic tables, and scenic overlook.

Enter Hog Rift. The rift is so-named because at one time a great number of hogs, fatally poisoned from eating distillery slop, were thrown into the river near here and their carcasses came to lodge along the river banks.

Class I + rapids begin at a diagonal ledge that extends from the New Jersey bank. A parallel ledge that reaches nearly across the river follows. Clear passage is possible around either end of the second ledge; openings in the ledge itself may be found by aiming for a conspicuous downstream "V." Rocks may protrude from the river at low water level.

One hundred yards downstream the river constricts at the last plunge of Hog Rift; clear passage with high standing waves near the Pennsylvania shore. New Jersey shore to center of river peppered with boulders; requires careful but quick maneuvers.

186.2. River passes through a small water gap, with high lime-stone bluffs on both sides.

185.7. A large gravel bar on the New Jersey side extends to the middle of the river. Passage to the right is clear.

185.0. Eddyside Park access area, maintained by the City of Easton, includes a concrete boat ramp, parking, sanitary facilities, trash disposal, fresh water, and a picnic area. There is also a swimming pool open to the public for a fee.

184.4. Easton Beachfront access area, maintained by the City of Easton. The city eventually hopes to develop a public beach and picnic area here. Presently there is a concrete boat ramp, trash disposal, and limited parking.

184.3. Getters Island begins. Its slender upstream tip nearly touchs the Pennsylvania bank.

The right channel is passable and ponded by a low dam at the downstream end of the island. A chute in the center of the dam makes an exciting quick drop into high standing waves. At moderately high water, the dam is submerged and should not be attempted due to a potentially dangerous hydraulic.

There is a Class I rapid in the main channel to the left of Getters Island. Shallows on both sides with the best route straight down the middle. Watch for boulders. Getters Island is named for Charles Getter, who was publicly executed at the site in 1833 for the murder of his wife.

184.1. Getters Island ends. Bushkill Creek enters, Pennsylvania side. This is the third "Bushkill Creek" to enter the Delaware River.

184.0. Pass beneath the Easton-Phillipsburg Toll Bridge. This single steel-truss span was constructed in 1938.

The city of Easton, Pennsylvania, the largest community on the Delaware River above Trenton, is on the right. Phillipsburg, New Jersey, is on the left. (See descriptions in the features section of this chapter.)

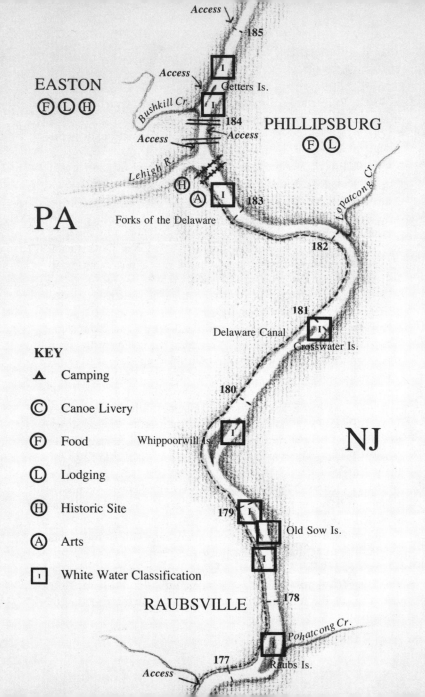

Access

185

EASTON
(F) (L) (H)

Access

Getters Is.

I

I

Bushkill Cr.

184

PHILLIPSBURG
(F) (L)

Access

Access

Lehigh R.

(H)

(A)

I

183

Lopatcong Cr.

PA

Forks of the Delaware

182

181

Delaware Canal

I

Crosswater Is.

180

Whippoorwill Is.

I

NJ

179

I

Old Sow Is.

I

KEY

▲ Camping

(C) Canoe Livery

(F) Food

(L) Lodging

(H) Historic Site

(A) Arts

I White Water Classification

RAUBSVILLE

178

Pohatcong Cr.

177

I

Access

Raubs Is.

Phillipsburg access area, maintained by the City of Phillipsburg, is on the New Jersey bank just downstream from the bridge. Includes parking, a boat ramp, trash disposal, and water.

183.9. Pass under North Hampton Street Bridge. One of the first bridges to span the Delaware, a wood structure with stone piers, was built at this site in 1806. The present bridge, with new abutments, was completed in 1895. Its cantilever-truss design is unique on the Delaware.

183.7. The Lehigh River enters, Pennsylvania side. The Lehigh, which drains a considerable area of northeast Pennsylvania, is one of the major tributaries of the Delaware. This is the Forks of the Delaware, a commercial and strategic prize for centuries and a main objective of the infamous Walking Purchase of 1737, which acquired the area from the Indians.

Easton Front Street Park access area, with a gravel boat ramp, parking, trash disposal and paid telephone, is just upstream from the confluence.

The Lehigh River falls over a 12-foot spillway just before entering the Delaware. This spillway was constructed to impound water for the Delaware Canal.

This is the site of Martin's Ferry, which plied the Delaware in the eighteenth century.

183.6. Hugh Moore Park and Canal Museum is on the bluff on the downstream side of the Forks. There are a dozen picnic tables with firegrills. The Delaware Canal begins here and parallels the river for 60 miles to tidewater at Bristol, Pennsylvania. (The features section of this chapter describes the Delaware Canal in more detail.)

Pass under Lehigh Valley Railroad Bridge.

183.5. Pass under double railroad bridge.

183.3. Begin Class I rapids, continuing .2 mile with no obstructions.

182.4. City of Easton wastewater treatment plant is on the bluff, Pennsylvania side. The outfall from the plant can be seen as a gray frothy discharge, which the river quickly assimilates. (For more information about pollution on the Delaware, see the section on water quality in the Introduction.)

181.9. Lopatcong Creek enters, New Jersey side. River bends sharply right.

181.0. Crosswater Island, a gravel bar with trees on the downstream end. At moderately low water level, the island touches the Pennsylvania shore.

A Class I rapid begins in the left channel at the head of the island and then continues nearly to the downstream end. There are no obstructions.

A small stream enters, New Jersey side, at the center of the island, creating a gravel bar that extends 15 yards into the river.

179.8. A large gravel bar on the left is followed immediately by Whippoorwill Island on the right. There is a strong Class I rapid that flows from right to left. No obstructions between the bar and island. The channel right of Whippoorwill Island is impassable at low water.

179.4. River bends sharply left downstream of Whippoorwill Island. There are numerous boat docks on the New Jersey shore for the next .4 mile.

178.9. Old Sow Island, with a broad gravel bar at its upstream end. A strong Class I rapid in the left channel flows around two small gravel bars. Passage is clear in the channel closest to Old Sow Island.

There is a rock ledge 100 yards downstream from the head of Old Sow Island in the right channel, extending from the Pennsylvania bank to the middle of the channel. Large standing waves below the ledge in the channel center. Class I rapid continues to the end of the island. Large gravel pits, New Jersey side.

178.4. Community of Raubsville, Pennsylvania shore. This is the site of Raub's Ferry, which plied the Delaware in the early nineteenth century.

177.6. Locks 22–23 on the Delaware Canal, Pennsylvania side. Wide wooden steps lead up the bank from the river to the towpath. There are picnic tables, firegrills, sanitary facilities, and a water pump. A white canal house stands at the river's edge just upstream from the wooden steps.

177.5. Raubs Island, also known as Groundhog Island. In moderately low water the Pennsylvania channel is dry. Pass under power lines.

177.4. A single concrete pylon stands in the center of Raubs Island. Begin Class I rapid.

177.3. Pohatcong Creek enters, New Jersey side, with large gravel bars extending to the middle of the channel. The current, pressed into a narrow channel, develops standing waves to 2 feet.

177.2. Raubs Island ends. River turns sharply right. Sharp rocky ledges protrude from water and extend from New Jersey shore. To old-time river raftsmen, who came downriver during spring floods, this formation was known as "Rocky Falls."

176.7. Fry Run Park access, operated by the North Hampton County Park Board. Limited parking, rough access, picnic tables, and a reconstructed historic stone-arch bridge. Access from U.S. Route 611.

Small stream enters, Pennsylvania side. River bends sharply left. There is a moderate current.

176.5. Angular rocks and ledges protrude from water for next .3 mile. Be alert for submerged boulders.

176.0. Limestone cliffs, New Jersey side.

175.5. A large gravel bar in the middle of the river.

175.4. A Class I rapid with no obstructions.

174.8. Pass under the Rieglesville Bridge. A wooden bridge was built here in 1835. The present two cable suspension bridge,

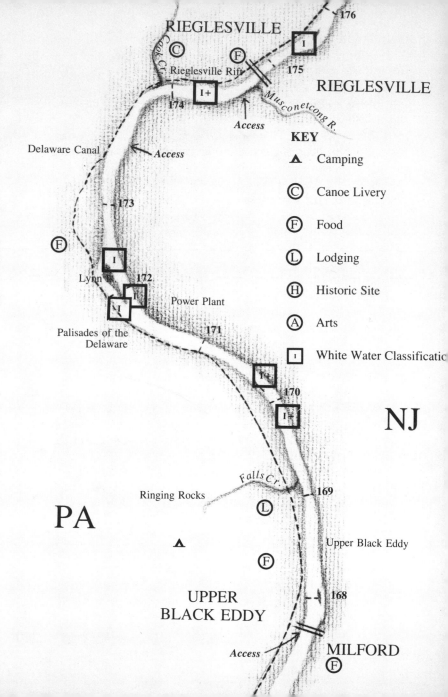

RIEGLESVILLE

176

175

RIEGLESVILLE

Rieglesville Rift

I+

174

Access

Delaware Canal

Access

Musconetcong R.

KEY

▲ Camping

Ⓒ Canoe Livery

Ⓕ Food

Ⓛ Lodging

Ⓗ Historic Site

Ⓐ Arts

☐ I White Water Classification

173

Ⓕ

I

Lynn

172

Power Plant

I

I

Palisades of the
Delaware

171

I+

170

I+

NJ

Falls Cr.

169

Ringing Rocks

Ⓛ

PA

Upper Black Eddy

▲

Ⓕ

UPPER
BLACK EDDY

168

Access

MILFORD

Ⓕ

Rieglesville suspension bridge, River Mile 174.8. Constructed in 1804. Photo by the author.

one of the most picturesque bridges to span the Delaware, was completed in 1904.

The communities of Rieglesville, Pennsylvania, and Rieglesville, New Jersey, stand at opposite ends of the bridge. There is rough access under the New Jersey end of the bridge.

174.7. Musconetcong River enters, New Jersey side. An abandoned Riegel Paper Company Plant stands along the river's edge just upstream from the Musconetcong.

174.6. Rieglesville access area, New Jersey side, owned by the Riegel Paper Company. A narrow boat ramp, limited parking, no other facilities.

174.4. Rieglesville Rift, a Class 1+ rapid, with a rocky ledge crossing the river diagonally downstream from the New Jersey side. There is a passable gap near the New Jersey shore, but the main current is near the Pennsylvania shore. At low water level the ledge itself cannot be penetrated, but at moderate level skilled canoeists can identify and pass through gaps.

173.9. Cook Creek enters, Pennsylvania side, with a gravel bar extending one-third of the way across the river. Lock 21 and the Durham Aqueduct of the Delaware Canal can be seen a short distance up Cook Creek. This was the site of Durham furnace, which produced iron from 1698 until 1908. Robert Durham, who operated the furnace here, developed the famous Durham boats that were used by George Washington in his crossing of the Delaware in 1776 and by tradesmen for many years along the river.

River is ponded for next 1.6 miles.

173.7. Holland Church access area, New Jersey side, maintained by the New Jersey Division of Fish, Game, and Shellfisheries. Rough access with limited parking and trash disposal.

172.3. Lynn Island. The main channel is on the left side of the island, with a Class I rapid. Rock ledges on the New Jersey bank are a possible hazard. A gravel bar extending from the New Jersey bank at the downstream end of Lynn Island constricts the river into another Class I rapid.

The channel to the right of Lynn Island is narrow but passable and enters from the Pennsylvania bank near the head of Lynn Island. Halfway down the channel a second small island is nestled near Lynn Island. A Class I rapid between the small island and the Pennsylvania shore requires some maneuvering around boulders.

171.9. Lynn Island ends. A large vegetated gravel bar lies in the center of the Pennsylvania channel, with a Class I rapids on either side.

Lock 20 on the Delaware Canal, with a few picnic tables nearby, is on the Pennsylvania bank.

The Palisades of the Delaware, also known as the "Narrows of

Nockamixen," rise 500 feet from the river on the Pennsylvania side. The palisades are composed of red sandstone and shale and are part of the Stockton Formation which extends into central Connecticut.

171.7. The Gilbert Generating Station, operated by New Jersey Power and Light Company, is on the New Jersey bank. Cooling water is discharged from a concrete outfall extending from the shore. Several high-tension lines cross the river in the vicinity.

171.0. Canoeists with vivid imaginations might see the profile of an Indian head in the rock formations atop the palisades.

170.2. A rock ledge extends from the New Jersey side. In very low water this ledge cannot be penetrated, and so canoeists must pass to the right. One hundred yards downstream a second ledge extends diagonally upstream from the New Jersey shore. There is a large boulder at the center of the ledge. Passage through the ledge may be obstructed, but it is sure near the Pennsylvania shore.

At moderate water level the river between 170.1 and 169.9 presents a Class I + rapid.

170.0. A rock ledge perpendicular to the flow in the middle of the river. The ledge itself presents a Class I rapid, but the channel is clear near either shore. There are many submerged and protruding rocks for the next .1 mile until a ledge that extends entirely across the river is encountered. The best passage here is in the middle or along the Pennsylvania shore.

169.0. Falls Creek enters, Pennsylvania side. Falls Creek may be followed upstream to Ringing Rocks. (See the features section of this chapter.)

The river flows into Upper Black Eddy.

167.7. Pass under Milford–Upper Black Eddy Bridge. The original wooden bridge was built in 1842; the present three-span steel truss was completed in 1933. The communities of Upper

Black Eddy, Pennsyvlania, and Milford, New Jersey, are at opposite ends of the bridge.

FEATURES

Easton, Pennsylvania/Phillipsburg, New Jersey

Except for Trenton, at the end of the canoeable Delaware River, Easton, Pennsylvania (population 26,027) is the largest community to be encountered on the banks of the river. Located at the strategic Forks of the Delaware, Easton was founded in 1752 by Thomas Penn, a son of William Penn. The site was acquired in the infamous Walking Purchase in 1737. Easton grew quickly as one of America's first industrial centers in the early nineteenth century. It was a meeting place of three canals—the Lehigh Canal which extended into the mountain coal fields, the Morris Canal which crossed New Jersey to the Hudson River, and the Delaware Canal which parallels the river to tidewater at Bristol. Five major railroads also came to Easton, making the city a hub of regional commerce.

Recently the people of Easton have made an effort to highlight the heritage of their city. Easton is part of the National Main Street Program, a special demonstration project of the National Trust for Historic Preservation. A self-guided walking tour takes visitors past more than 30 buildings remarkable for their historic interest or architecture, ranging from a tavern built in 1754 to art deco commercial buildings. In Center Square, only two blocks from the river, an outdoor farmers' market operates every Tuesday, Thursday, and Saturday.

Easton offers all the services to be expected in a city of its size.

There are numerous restaurants from fast food to fancy fare, shopping centers, movie theaters, several motels, and cultural activities. For specific information contact the Two Rivers Area Commerce Council, 157 South Fourth Street, Easton, Pennsylvania 18042, 215/253–4211.

Phillipsburg, New Jersey, population 16,647, stands immediately across the river from Easton. The Phillipsburg area was sparsely settled until 1832 when the Morris Canal was opened, linking the Delaware River with the Hudson River at Newark. Phillipsburg became a seaport 60 miles from tidewater, and it grew further with the arrival of railroads in 1852. The canal is long gone, yet Phillipsburg remains an important regional center. There are numerous grocery stores, restaurants, a motel, and shops within walking distance from the river.

The Delaware Canal

The boom days of towpath canals were largely over by the turn of the century. The greater efficiency and speed of railroads made it impossible for the canals to compete. By 1930 most of the old canals were long abandoned and in ruins. But today there are many people living in the Pennsylvania communities along the Delaware River below Easton who readily recall the barges loaded with lumber and coal that once plied the Delaware Canal. The canal, which connected Easton and tidewater at Bristol, was operated commercially until 1931, outlasting all the other towpath canals in America.

Beginning with construction of the Erie Canal in 1825, the road to westward expansion was paved with water. Over the next several decades about 4,000 miles of towpath canals were constructed in eastern America, enabling the tentacles of commerce to penetrate the wilderness. Pennsylvania alone had 1200 miles of

canals, more than any other state. The Mainline Canal from Philadelphia to Pittsburgh, the Union Canal along the Schuylkill River,
and the Delaware and Hudson Canal (which crosses into New
York at Lackawaxen) were all part of this extensive system. In
1829 the Lehigh Canal was completed from the coal country of
the Pocono Mountains to Easton. The Delaware Canal, completed
in 1832, in turn connected Easton to the tidewater Delaware River
at Bristol. Hardrock coal mined in the mountains could be barged
to market at Philadelphia in a few days. During the peak years in
the mid-nineteenth century, over 3,000 boats travelled over the
canal annually. Ultimately, about 33 million tons of coal and 6
million tons of other cargoes would be mule-barged to market.

Life on the canal was hard from the beginning. The canal was
constructed mostly by Irish immigrants and local farmers on con-
tract, who worked only with hand tools and occasionally with
horses. Workdays were long, pay was low, and the labor strenu-
ous. Each barge was a standard 87½ feet long, by 10½ feet wide
and drew 5 feet of water when loaded. The barge was piloted by a
crew of two, often husband and wife. A team of two mules, walking ahead on the towpath, pulled the barge along the canal. The
crew would stop only to rest the mules or to exchange teams. The
locktenders, who lived in company houses adjacent to the canal,
were on call around the clock to pass traffic through the locks.

Soon after the canal was abandoned, it became used increasingly for recreation. Fishing, canoeing, and travelling on party
barges became regular activities on the canal. In 1940 the State of
Pennsylvania established the Theodore Roosevelt State Park
which encompassed the Delaware Canal.

Because it was commercially operated and maintained as late as
1931, the Delaware Canal remains in excellent condition along its
60-mile course. The canal is never more than a few hundred yards
from the Delaware River, and in places it is separated from the

river only by an earthen berm. Numerous points of interest along the canal are easily accessible from the Delaware River. The canal can be used to make a "circle" canoe trip, which involves paddling downstream on the river and then returning upstream by canal to the starting point. There is a slight current in the canal, but this can be countered easily in a canoe.

The best place to learn about the canal is the Hugh Moore State Park and Canal Museum at Easton. Access to the museum is easily made just downstream from the confluence of the Delaware and Lehigh Rivers. The museum contains several excellent exhibits including a full size mock-up of a barge cabin, a gallery of canal art, implements and tools used in canal operation, scale models of canal construction, and an old movie of mules pulling a barge through a lock. (The movie should not be missed.) There is a $1.00 admission fee. The museum is at the canal's starting point, and the principal gate lock is just outside.

There are 23 lift locks along the canal, most of which are operational. The lift locks, which were used to raise and lower boats between different water levels, consist of narrow stone channels with massive wooden gates at both ends. The water level in the channel could be raised or lowered to bring the barge in line with the adjacent canal section. Several of these locks may be visited easily from the river, including Durham Lock at Mile 173.8; Narrows Lock at Mile 171.9; Lewis Lock at Mile 160.5; Whites Double Lock at Mile 156.8 (just below Point Pleasant); Lumberville Lock at Mile 155.5 (slightly upstream from the Lumberville Foot Bridge); and Locks 9, 10, and 11 at Mile 148, which raise the canal level along Wells Falls at New Hope. The remaining locks, of course, may be found by canoeing or walking along the canal itself.

In numerous places the canal had to cross streams and rivers. For this purpose aqueducts were constructed to contain the canal as it bridged a stream below. Some of the aqueducts that may be seen include Durham Aqueduct, which is partially dismantled, at Mile 173.8; Gallows Run Aqueduct, by Lynn Island, at Mile 172.1; Tinicum Creek Aqueduct, one of the highest, at Mile 161.6; Tohicon Creek Aqueduct at Point Pleasant, Mile 157.0; Stony Run Aqueduct at Mile 144.0; and Brock Creek Aqueduct at Yardley, which may be seen by paddling a short distance up Brock Creek, Mile 138.0.

Mule-drawn barge rides are open to the public in New Hope every day between Memorial Day and Labor Day. Passenger barges are hauled up the canal 4½ miles, then returned to New Hope. The rides makes for a different and relaxing side trip and gives passengers a taste of what life may have been like on the old Delaware Canal.

Ringing Rocks

Atop the Palisades of the Delaware near Upper Black Eddy is an exposure of angular boulders. No soil has developed in this four-acre clearing, nor has any vegetation taken root. The field of boulders has an artificial appearance, as if it were placed there on purpose by the working of hundreds of dump trucks. But the exposure is entirely natural, and when the rocks in this clearing are struck with a hammer, they ring like bells. This curiosity has been long known as Ringing Rocks, and a county park has been established here to protect the site.

When J. Wallace Hoff canoed the Delaware in 1892 he characterized Ringing Rocks as "a collection of metallic boulders that emit ringing and even musical combinations upon being struck." Indeed, with a few friends, simple melodies can be played by striking different rocks at the right time. As a rule, the larger boulders produce bass tones, while smaller ones are treble. The Ringing

Ringing Rocks, near Upper Black Eddy. Musical tones are produced when rocks are struck with a hammer. This four-acre phenomenon can be reached by a one-mile hike from the Delaware. Photo by the author.

Rocks are composed of rather fine conglomerate stone. Though some have suggested that a metallic content is responsible for the resonance, it is more likely that interior stress caused by repeated freezing and thawing produces the bell-like tones.

Ringing Rocks can be reached from the river in two ways. The easiest one involves walking up Bridgeton Hill Road (which intersects Pennsylvania Route 32 .2 mile above the Upper Black Eddy–Milford Bridge) .8 mile to Ringing Rocks Road, then turning right, and continuing .2 mile to the park entrance. A more adventurous route requires bushwhacking up Falls Creek, an intermittent stream that flows into the Delaware at Mile 169.0. (Caution: Another small stream meets the Delaware immediately upstream from the confluence of the Delaware and Falls Creek; Falls Creek, unlike its neighbor, intersects the Delaware Canal and Pennsylvania Route 32 a short distance from the river). The stream tumbles over a series of sandstone and shale ledges through a deep hemlock ravine that ends upstream at a solid rock wall. A wide trail to the right of the wall leads to the Ringing Rocks.

CAMPING AND SERVICES

Camping

The land adjacent to the river and the river islands is mostly privately owned. There are many good places to pitch a tent, however, and canoeists who ask permission are often allowed to stay.

1. A few primitive campsites, available by permission only, are maintained by the Pennsylvania Power and Light Company at its Martins Creek access area, Mile 193.4. A gate leading to the access area is closed and locked at night.
2. Ringing Rocks Family Campground (R.D. 1, Box 141, Upper Black Eddy, Pennsylvania 18972, 215/982-5552) is located on Woodland Drive about one mile up the hill from Upper Black Eddy. There are 75 campsites, modern sanitary facilities with showers, a playground for children, and a camp store.

Canoe Liveries

Point Pleasant Canoes, one of the largest Delaware River outfitters, operates two bases in this section. PPC offers individual rentals and group packages anywhere on the river. Recently PPC has been featuring raft and inner tube excursions.

1. Point Pleasant Canoes, Martins Creek base (Box 154B, R. D. 1, Easton, Pennsylvania 18042, 215/258-2606), located at River Mile 189.8.
2. Point Pleasant Canoes, Rieglesville base (Box 304, Rieglesville, Pennsylvania 18077, 215/749-2093), at River Mile 174.0, access from U.S. Route 611.

Other Services

The cities of Easton, Pennsylvania, and Phillipsburg, New Jersey, are discussed in the features section of this chapter. Other services available in this general area are listed below:

190.6 Martins Creek, Pennsylvania. The Pub Dining Room and Restaurant, two outside pay phones.

189.0 Martins Creek, Pennsylvania. Serendipity Motel and General Store, a short climb up the riverbank.

185.6 Outskirts of Easton, Pennsylvania. General store, ice available.

174.8 Rieglesville, Pennsylvania. The historic Rieglesville Hotel, constructed in 1838, stands at the end of the Rieglesville Bridge. Joe's Pizza and Diana's Family Restaurant are within ¼ mile of the river.

174.8 Rieglesville, New Jersey. A small tavern with ice available is located at the end of the Rieglesville Bridge.

172.3 Rieglesville, Pennsylvania. Uncle Andy's Steak and Ale House is located at the junction of Pennsylvania Route 32 and Route 611 (from Lynn Island, .3 mile north on Pennsylvania Route 32). A snack bar with ice cream and soda is adjacent to Uncle Andy's.

168.6 Upper Black Eddy, Pennsylvania. The Upper Black Eddy Inn, between the Delaware Canal and the river, was a favorite with river raftsmen and canal bargemen. Today it is a fine restaurant.

168.0 Upper Black Eddy, Pennsylvania. Upper Black Eddy General Store. Travel ¼ mile north of the Upper Black Eddy Bridge on Pennsylvania Route 32; then turn left and continue 100 yards on a side road.

167.7 Upper Black Eddy, Pennsylvania. The Bridgetown House, a fine restaurant, is located at the end of the Upper Black Eddy Bridge. Ice and soda are available at a nearby gas station.

167.5 Milford, New Jersey. The village contains the Del-Val Market, Davies Pizza and Restaurant, the Old Mill Ford Oyster House, and several antique and gift shops.

Upper Black Eddy to Lambertville

The river passes through 19 miles of mixed forests and farmlands. The rolling hills are characteristic of the Piedmont geophysical province, and outcrops of sandstone and shale rock tower above the river in places. Generally, the river is very shallow, with long gentle pools separated by mild rapids. There are no severe rifts in this section, though rapids at the end of Prahis Island and at the Lumberville wing dams offer excitement. A 2½-mile-long maze of islands beginning at Mile 162.6 provides many narrow channels to be explored.

Pennsylvania Route 32 and the Delaware Canal run parallel and very close to the river on the Pennsylvania side. The historic vilages of Upper Black Eddy, Erwinna, Point Pleasant, Lumberville, and New Hope are nestled along the riverbank. Several genteel inns dating from the early nineteenth century can be found along Route 32. Most of the old inns offer lodging and a style of hospitality that has long disappeared in most of the country.

New Jersey Route 29 closely follows the river. The Delaware and Raritan Feeder Canal begins at Bulls Island, then parallels the river to Lambertville and beyond. The D&R Canal as well as the Delaware Canal in Pennsylvania can be used for circle canoe trips, which involve canoeing downstream on the river, then paddling upstream on the canal to the starting point. The communities of Milford, Frenchtown, Stockton, and Lambertville began as ferry points on the river and retain a distinct historical flavor.

RIVER GUIDE

167.7. Pass under the Milford–Upper Black Eddy Bridge, a three-truss iron bridge built in 1933. The concrete and rubble abutments present today are from the original wooden bridge, which was built here in 1842.

The community of Upper Black Eddy is on the Pennsylvania shore. Upper Black Eddy was an important stop on the Delaware Canal and a popular stopping place for timber raftsmen in the eighteenth and nineteenth centuries. The old Upper Black Eddy Inn still stands between the river and canal, .8 mile upstream from the bridge. The community of Milford, New Jersey, is at the eastern end of the bridge.

Upper Black Eddy access area, maintained by the Pennsylvania Fish Commission, is on the Pennsylvania bank just downstream from the bridge. There is ample parking, a boat ramp, sanitary facilities, and trash disposal. Access from Pennsylvania Route 32.

167.2. A small stream enters, New Jersey side. Gravel bars at the mouth of the stream extend about 20 yards into the river.

167.0. A small grassy island is in the middle right of the river.

The smokestacks and water tower of the Riegel Paper Company's Milford plant can be seen on the New Jersey side. Riegel Paper is one of the major industries along the Delaware River, producing printing, packaging, and specialty papers.

166.9. Elongated small island with a few trees in the middle of the river.

166.8. Hakihokake Creek enters, New Jersey side, with gravelly shallows near the mouth of the stream. Another small round island, middle right of river.

166.6. A small elongate island, right side of river.

A very mild riffle, marking the end of Upper Black Eddy.

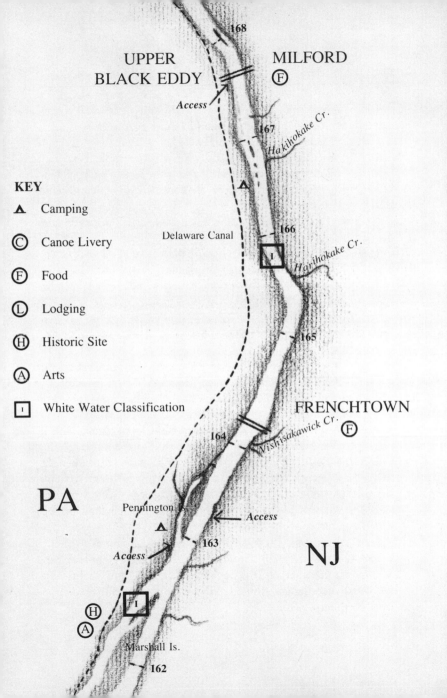

166.5. An elongate grassy island, right side of river. May be submerged at moderately high water level.

166.0. Pass under high-tension line.

165.7. A Class I rapid begins with a submerged ledge extending diagonally downstream from the New Jersey bank, then a second ledge straight across the river about 40 yards downstream. Best passage is left to center.

Harihokake Creek enters, New Jersey side, with grassy gravel bars extending downstream.

165.4. River bends slightly right. Moderate riffle across river, with minor obstructions on the extreme left.

165.0. Rocky ledges along New Jersey shore extend into the river for next .2 mile.

164.3. Pass under Uhlertown–Frenchtown Bridge. A wooden bridge was first built here in 1843. The present six-span steel truss was erected in 1931 on the original abutments and piers. The town of Frenchtown, New Jersey, originally called Alexandria, is on the left. Uhlertown, Pennsylvania, formerly known as Mexico, was a whistle-stop on the Delaware Canal. There are several interesting old buildings dating from the canal's heyday.

164.2. Nishisakawick Creek enters, New Jersey side, with a large gravel bar extending nearly to the middle of the river.

163.8. Mile-long Pennington island begins on the extreme right side of the river. The narrow channel along the Pennsylvania shore is passable in a canoe at moderate water level. A private camp maintained by the Presbyterian Church is located on the island—no trespassing.

163.7. An increase in river current, not amounting to a riffle.

163.4. Kingman public access area, New Jersey shore, operated by the New Jersey Division of Fish, Game, and Shellfisheries. Trash disposal and limited parking; no other facilities. Access from New Jersey Route 29.

163.0. Pennington Island ends.

162.9. Tinicum County Park access area, Pennsylvania side, maintained by the Bucks County Department of Parks and Recreation. A concrete boat ramp, parking, trash disposal, telephones, water, and sanitary facilities. Access from Pennsylvania Route 32.

162.5. Beginning of Marshalls Island, which extends nearly 2 miles downstream, in the middle of the river. Marshalls was once known as Man-of-War Island because tall trees on the upstream end resembled the masts of a battleship. The island's current name is derived from the Marshall family, which included Edward Marshall, one of the runners participating in the infamous Walking Purchase of 1737. Marshalls Island is owned by the Boy Scouts.

Marshalls Island begins a complex maze of 11 islands that extends 2½ miles along the Delaware. Exploring the little channels among the islands is an adventure in itself. Access to these channels is somewhat easier from the left side of Marshalls Island.

162.4. Right of Marshalls Island. The Old Stover Mill, built in 1832 and one of the earliest turbine-wheel mills in the country, stands at the very edge of the river on the Pennsylvania bank. The mill is now maintained as a museum, library, and art gallery.

A rocky ledge extends from the base of the mill to the tip of a large gravel bar in the center of the channel, making for a Class I rapid. At low water the ledge can be breached only at its center.

161.5. Tinicum Creek enters, Pennsylvania side. A high aqueduct of the Delaware Canal crosses Tinicum Creek about 50 yards from the river. A large gravel bar extends into the river channel.

Pinkertons Island begins, left channel.

161.3. The Devils Tea Table, a pedestal-shaped rock formation high on the sandstone cliffs on the New Jersey bank. Devils Tea Table is on private property, closed to hikers.

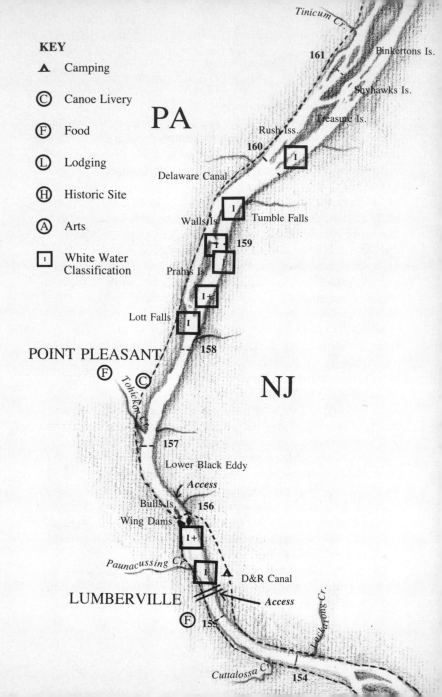

KEY

△ Camping

Ⓒ Canoe Livery

Ⓕ Food

Ⓛ Lodging

Ⓗ Historic Site

Ⓐ Arts

□ I White Water Classification

PA

NJ

Tinicum Cr.

161

Pinkertons Is.

Shyhawks Is.

Treasure Is.

Rush Iss.

160

Delaware Canal

Walls/Is.

Tumble Falls

159

Prahis Is.

Lott Falls

158

POINT PLEASANT

Ⓕ   Ⓒ

Tohickon Cr.

157

Lower Black Eddy

Access

Bulls Is.

Wing Dams

156

I+

Paunacussing Cr.

I

LUMBERVILLE

D&R Canal

Access

Ⓕ 155

Lockatong Cr.

Cuttalossa Cr.

154

On clear days canoeists often see antique biplanes, home-builts, gliders, ultralights, and other unusual aircraft flying over the Delaware. These originate from Van Sant Airport, a grass strip 2 miles from the river in Pennsylvania.

Shyhawks Island begins, left channel.

160.8. End Marshall Island; begin Treasure Island. The narrow channel separating the islands, which leads diagonally downstream from the left side, is spanned by a precarious wooden suspension bridge. Mild riffles in both left and right channels around Treasure Island.

160.7. Treasure Island is owned by the Philadelphia Council of the Boy Scouts of America and is operated as a summer camp. The scouts are ferried from the Pennsylvania shore to the island on a little cable ferry reminiscent of the scows used to cross the Delaware in the nineteenth century.

160.4. A small stream enters, New Jersey side. Mild riffle in left channel.

160.2. Treasure Island ends. There are moderate riffles near the island on both sides.

Rush Islands, extending .2 mile downstream, begin in left center and right center of the river, forming three channels: Pennsylvania, middle, and New Jersey.

160.1. A Class I rapid, New Jersey and middle channels. A rocky ledge extends to the middle of the channel from the New Jersey shore.

159.3 River bends widely left. A series of shale ledges extends from the New Jersey shore nearly across the river. At moderate water level it is possible to maneuver through the various clefts between the ledges. In slightly higher water, the ledges are submerged and present a Class I rapid known as Tumble Falls. The river channel from the middle to the Pennsylvania bank is always passable.

Begin Walls Island in the middle of the river. A moderate riffle in the right channel.

159.1. A narrow channel between Walls Island and Prahis Island, diagonally left from Pennsylvania channel. A Class I rapid with high standing waves is in the channel.

Three rocky ledges cross the left channel in the next .2 mile, making a series of Class I rapids.

158.3. In left channel beginning of elongate island surrounded by wide gravel bars.

Right channel: Lott Falls, a Class I+ rapid requiring quick maneuvers around rocks and ledges.

158.2. End Prahis Island.

Left channel: Begin Class I rapid extending .1 mile to end of gravel bar. Standing waves to 2 feet can be found in the right center of the channel.

157.2. Point Pleasant Canoes, one of the giant outfitters on the Delaware River, operates its main base on the Pennsylvania bank. Private canoes may be launched for a fee.

Three piers of the old Point Pleasant Bridge stand in the river. The bridge was washed out in the 1955 hurricane.

157.0. Tohickon Creek enters, Pennsylvania side. Tohickon Creek is dam-controlled; in the spring and at dam releases, it contains Class III and IV rapids for kayakers and rafters. Otherwise it is too shallow for any kind of boat. Gravel bars upstream and downstream from the creek mouth extend almost to the middle of the river.

Point Pleasant was once an important stop on the Delaware Canal. Today there are numerous antique shops and galleries here.

Point Pleasant is the proposed location for a pumped diversion of the Delaware River to supply water to Bucks and Montgomery County, Pennsylvania. Much of this water would be used to cool the nuclear power plant at Limerick. Although the DRBC says

Lumberville. Public sentiment runs against construction of a pumped diversion of the Delaware. Photo by the author.

that only 2 percent of the river's flow would be diverted, the proposal has generated great opposition in the surrounding communities. Opponents contend that reduction of the Delaware's flow would crimp recreational activities and have adverse effects on the river ecosystem. Signs like "Dump the Pump" and "Dehydration Without Representation Is Tyranny" can be spotted on homes and businesses from Trenton to Easton.

156.9. River begins a wide turn to the left, entering Lower Black Eddy.

156.8. Numerous boat docks and swimming rafts for summer homes for next .4 mile. There are many motorboats active in this area. Canoeists should stay near the shore.

156.1. Byron public access area, New Jersey side. Operated and maintained by Delaware and Raritan Canal State Park. A gravel ramp with parking and trash disposal, access from New Jersey Route 29.

156.0. Begin Bulls Island, New Jersey side. The channel between the New Jersey shore and Bulls Island is the intake to the Delaware and Raritan Feeder Canal. (See features section of this chapter.) By paddling down the lefthand channel, canoeists will reach the D&R Canal gate lock in .7 mile. There is a canoe launch and landing on the canal where the park road crosses. Canoes can be carried easily across Bulls Island from the canal to the river and vice versa.

Bulls Island is owned by the New Jersey State Park Service and is operated as a campground by Delaware and Raritan Canal State Park.

155.9. The Lumberville wing dams, originally constructed to impound water to feed the D&R Canal, extend from both banks to a gap in the middle of the river. The river flows through the gap in a safe but very exciting Class I to II rapid. There is a precipitous drop-off, followed by standing waves up to 3 feet high.

Water fails to go over the wing dams only when the river is very low. Canoeists should never attempt to go over the dams—there is a potentially dangerous hydraulic at the base—but must pass through the center opening. To avoid passage through the Lumberville wing dam, canoeists may paddle down the channel on the New Jersey side of Bulls Island to the D&R Canal, then carry their boat across the island back to the river.

155.6. A Class I rapid with a few boulders. Paunacussing Creek enters, Pennsylvania side, with large gravel bars extending to the center of the river. The Delaware Canal crosses the creek in an aqueduct.

155.4. A rough dirt trail leads up the Pennsylvania bank to lock 12 on the Delaware Canal. There are picnic tables and firegrills at this site.

The Lumberville-Raven Rocks Pedestrian Bridge. Constructed in 1947. The Delaware Canal and towpath are in the foreground. Photo by the author.

155.3. Pass under Lumberville–Raven Rocks Pedestrian Bridge, one of the most picturesque structures to span the Delaware. A wooden bridge was built at this site in 1853; it was condemned and closed in 1945. The present suspension bridge was built by John A. Roebling & Sons Company in 1947 on the original piers and abutments.

At the Pennsylvania end of the bridge stands a two-story stone house, built in 1853, which was used for many years by toll collectors. Immediately downstream from the bridge the famous Black Bass Hotel overlooks the canal and the river.

Bulls Island access area is just downstream from the bridge on Bulls Island. Maintained by the New Jersey State Park Service, it has parking, a boat ramp, picnic areas, water, sanitary facilities, trash disposal, and telephones. Access from New Jersey Route 29.

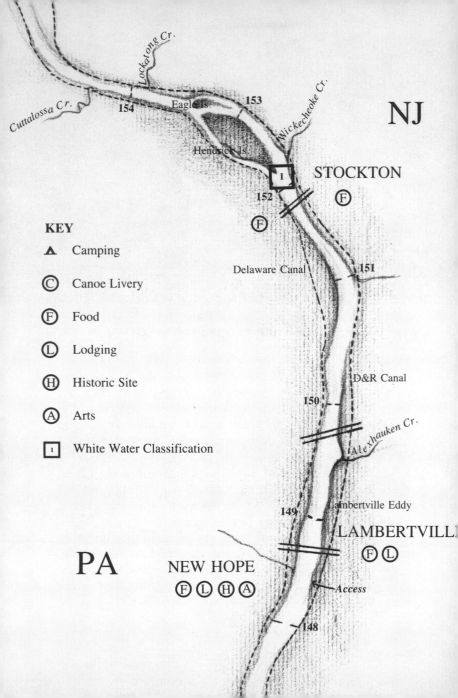

155.0. Wide gravel bar extends from Bulls Island.

154.8. Bulls Island ends. River begins wide turn to the left.

154.3. Cuttalossa Creek enters, Pennsylvania side.

153.9. Lockatong Creek enters, New Jersey side.

153.4. Begin Eagle Island in center of river. A riffle with a few boulders is in the left channel.

153.3. Begin Hendrick Island, to the right of Eagle Island. The channel between the islands is passable, but the passage between Hendrick Island and the Pennsylvania shore is very narrow and not navigable at low water level.

152.4. Wickecheoke Creek enters, New Jersey side. Historic Smith's Mill, also known as Prallsville Mill, with its scenic spillway can be seen at the mouth of the creek. A typical nineteenth-century gristmill, Smith's Mill is part of D&R Canal State Park and is open to the public on Sundays and for special events. The D&R canal crosses Wickecheoke Creek in an aqueduct.

152.2. End of Hendrick Island. A Class I rapid consisting of three submerged ledges with riffles in between.

151.8. Pass under Center Bridge. This six-span crossing was constructed in 1926 on piers and abutments originally built in 1814. A wooden bridge built that year lasted until 1924 when it was destroyed by fire. This is the site of Reading's Ferry, which began regular crossings in 1711 and which was the first commercial ferry on the Delaware.

The community of Stockton, New Jersey, stands at the east end of the bridge.

149.8. Pass under high-tension line.

149.7. Pass under New Hope–Lambertville Toll Bridge, carrying U.S. Route 202. This bridge was completed in 1971.

149.6. Large gravel bar near Pennsylvania shore.

149.5. Alexhauken Creek enters, New Jersey side. A large gravel bar extends one-quarter of the way across river.

Historic Smith's Mill at Prallsville. Seen from the Delaware at River Mile 152.4. The Delaware and Raritan Feeder Canal crosses Wickecheoke Creek in an aqueduct. Photo by the author.

Enter Lambertville Eddy, extending to Wells Falls at Mile 148.0. Many motorboats and waterskiers use this eddy. Canoeists should stay near the shore.

148.7. Pass under New Hope–Lambertville Bridge. A wooden bridge built at this site in 1814 was destroyed by the flood of 1903. The present six-span steel structure was built in 1904 on the original piers.

FEATURES

The Delaware and Raritan Canal

In 1676 William Penn proposed the idea of connecting New York and Philadelphia by a canal across New Jersey. It was not until 1830, however, that the Delaware and Raritan Canal Company was chartered to construct the waterway. The canal opened to barge traffic in 1834, with tidewater locks on the Raritan River at New Brunswick and on the Delaware River at Bordentown. To provide water at a sufficient level for the canal at Trenton, a feeder canal was built along the Delaware River from Bulls Island to Trenton.

The feeder canal was not built as a waterway for boats, but as a water conduit. Even so, the feeder canal was navigable by canal barges and was an important means of transportation in Stockton, Lambertville, and Titusville in the nineteenth century. In the 1840s the locks at Lambertville were improved, allowing access from the Delaware River. Barges brought coal from the mountains of Pennsylvania, travelled down the Delaware Canal, crossed the river above Wells Falls, and entered the D&R Canal. From there coal could be barged to market at Trenton and other communities in central New Jersey.

The D&R Canal was constructed mostly by the hands of Irish immigrant workers. In 1832 a deadly epidemic swept through the labor camps. Many workers were buried in unmarked graves along the canal, with one mass grave at Bulls Island. The canal itself, which has already survived 150 years, remains as a monument to these laborers: the hand-laid drywalls that retain the canal water and the precision masonry of the canal locks testify to the quality workmanship that went into the canal.

The Delaware and Raritan Canal suffered the same fate as the other towpath canals in America, succumbing to competition from the more efficient railroads. Indeed after 1871 the Pennsylvania Railroad took a lease on the canal and operated it until the early 1930s. But even though the D&R Canal closed to navigation after 99 years of barge traffic, it is today a profit-making operation. Delaware River water carried by the canal is sold to communities and industries throughout central New Jersey. Most of the water control devices on the canal — locks, flumes, gates — have been modified for the canal's modern use as a water supply aqueduct. As a result, the D&R Canal continues to be maintained and is in excellent condition along its 60-mile length.

The D&R Feeder Canal closely parallels the Delaware River between the gate lock at Bulls Island and the Scudders Falls Bridge above Trenton. The towpath and canal are in excellent condition along the way. The canal is an excellent place for beginning canoeists to practice and explore. Circle trips are possible by paddling downstream on the river, then returning upstream on the D&R Canal to the starting point. There are several low bridges and two locks which must be portaged around on the canal between Bulls Island and Scudders Falls.

CAMPING AND SERVICES

Camping

Lands bordering the river, except as noted below, are private, and permission must be secured before camping. Most of the other river islands are also private; canoe campers are not welcome.

1. Dog Wood Haven Campground (R.D. 1, Box 615, Lodi Hill Rd., Upper Black Eddy, Pennsylvania 18972, 215/ 982–5402), at Mile 166.5, is accessible from the Upper

Black Eddy access area on the Pennsylvania bank. Dog Wood Haven is operated by Pennsylvania's Roosevelt State Park and has a limited number of sites available with picnic tables and charcoal grills.

2. Bulls Island (R.D. 2, Box 417, Stockton, New Jersey 08559, 609/397–2949), at Mile 156 is the last public camping area on the Delaware and is part of New Jersey's D&R Canal State Park. About 100 individual campsites are nestled under the tall trees and along the river bank. Each site has a picnic table and firepit. There are new sanitary facilities with showers, a playground, and drinking water. Just upstream from the wing dam a swimming area is open. (Swim at your own risk.) Camping at Bulls Island is on a "site available" basis; campers select their site, then register and pay a fee at the office. Campsites begin at the upstream end of the island and continue to the pedestrian bridge at Mile 155.3. The park office is located on the road leading to the pedestrian bridge.

3. Tinicum County Park Campground, with picnic tables, fresh water, grills, and sanitary facilities, is on the Delaware Canal at the Tinicum access area, Mile 163.0.

Canoe Livery

Point Pleasant Canoes (P.O. Box 6, Point Pleasant, Pennsylvania 18950, 215/297–8400/8949), one of the giants of Delaware River recreation, operates its main base at River Mile 157.3. PPC, which has 1,000 canoes at four bases, offers individual rentals and group packages, including portage, anywhere on the river. Recently PPC has also been featuring rafts and innertubes in this section of the Delaware. The pale blue Point Pleasant Canoe buses are a familiar sight on the roads paralleling the river.

Other Services

Several historic inns, some dating from the eighteenth century, are located along the Delaware River and Canal on Pennsylvania Route 32, which was originally a stagecoach line. These inns were favored by timber raftsmen and canal bargemen, and today are open as restaurant-hotels offering a distinctive atmosphere.

164.3 Uhlertown, Pennsylvania. The Farmer's Daughter Farm Market operates during the summer at the Pennsylvania end of the Frenchtown Bridge.

162.7 Erwinna, Pennsylvania. River Road Gallery and Farm; specialty and gift shops in a cluster on Pennsylvania Route 32.

162.2 Erwinna, Pennsylvania. The Golden Pheasant Inn.

157.1 Point Pleasant, Pennsylvania. Home of Point Pleasant Canoes' main base. PPC charges $1.00 for customer parking, and $5.00 to launch a private canoe. Across the Delaware Canal from the canoe base is the Point Pleasant Village store where sandwiches, soda, ice cream, and ice are available. One hundred yards further south on Pennsylvania Route 32 is a little store called the Trading Post and a U.S. Post Office.

156.4 Point Pleasant, Pennsylvania. The Walking Treaty Inn, another historic Pennsylvania inn. Outside public phone.

155.4 Lumberville, Pennsylvania. The Black Bass Hotel, located at the end of the pedestrian bridge, renowned for fine dinners and sophisticated charm. A windowed dining room overlooks the river.

155.3 Lumberville, Pennsylvania. The Lumberville General Store is located 100 yards south of the footbridge on Pennsylvania Route 32. The store also serves as a post office and has bicycles for rent for use along the Delaware Canal and the nearby country roads.

151.8 Pennsylvania. The Center Bridge Inn is located on the traffic circle at the Pennsylvania end of the Stockton Bridge. Dilly's Ice Cream Corner, with a take-out window, picnic tables, and pay phone, is also located on the traffic circle.

151.8 Stockton, New Jersey. Located at the end of the Stockton Bridge. Le Bistro Restaurant is 100 yards from the bridge. Colligan's Stockton Inn, at the intersection of New Jersey Route 29 and Stockton's Main Street, has been listed by *New Jersey Magazine* as one of the finest restaurants in the state. Several antique shops are also located in Stockton.

Lambertville to Trenton

This section begins with Wells Falls, the most severe rapid on the Delaware, and ends at Trenton Falls, which marks the boundary of tidewater. The river continues through the Piedmont geophysical province until Trenton Falls. Trenton Falls is on the "fall line," that is, the boundary between the Piedmont and the Coastal Plain provinces. Since the Piedmont is composed of solid rock and the Coastal Plain consists of uncemented sand and clay, the fall line causes severe rapids in most eastern rivers. The Great Falls of the Potomac near Washington, D.C., is a striking example. Below Trenton Falls the Delaware flows 133 miles through the Coastal Plain to the mouth of the river at Delaware Bay.

The lands along the river are increasingly urbanized in this section, starting with Lambertville and New Hope at the beginning, then Titusville, Washington Crossing, West Trenton, Yardley, Morrisville, and Trenton itself. Most of the way, however, the riverbank is lined with trees, and the scenery is not unpleasant. For the last mile above tidewater, the river is channeled between high concrete embankments.

At Wells Falls and Scudders Falls the river is funneled through wing dams. Canoeists should never paddle over the dams, but should aim for the center chute. Wells Falls is so severe that novices are advised to detour the rapids on the D&R Canal or the Delaware Canal. At extreme low tide the last ledges of Trenton Falls present hazardous rapids that should be avoided by all but the most experienced canoeists.

Pennsylvania Route 32 and New Jersey Route 29 parallel the river closely on either side. The Delaware Canal continues along the riverbank in Pennsylvania, in places swerving away from the river, while the Delaware and Raritan Canal in New Jersey is very near the river for the first 10 miles. Either canal makes for good circle trips; by paddling down the river, then returning back upstream on the canal.

One of the most important events in American history took place on this section of the Delaware. In 1776 George Washington led his tired troops across the river for a surprise attack on the Hessian garrison at Trenton. This victory revitalized the Revolutionary cause. Both New Jersey and Pennsylvania have established state parks to commemorate the event, and the two parks are well worth a visit from the river.

Below Trenton the Delaware River is affected by the twice-daily surge of tides from the Atlantic Ocean. The river becomes much deeper and much more polluted. Oil tankers, freight barges, garbage scows, and other heavy shipping use the river for access to the industrial cities that line it. Though motorboating and sailing are popular in some areas, the Delaware below Trenton is not well-suited for canoeing.

There are four public access areas in this section: Lambertville, just above Wells Falls; Belle Mountain at Mile 146.8; Yardley at Mile 138.7; and Mercer County, 1½ miles below Trenton Falls in the tidewater Delaware.

RIVER GUIDE

148.7. Pass under the New Hope–Lambertville Bridge, a six-span steel truss built in 1904. A wooden bridge erected here in 1814 was destroyed in the flood of 1903. The present bridge rests upon the original masonry piers. (For descriptions of Lambert-

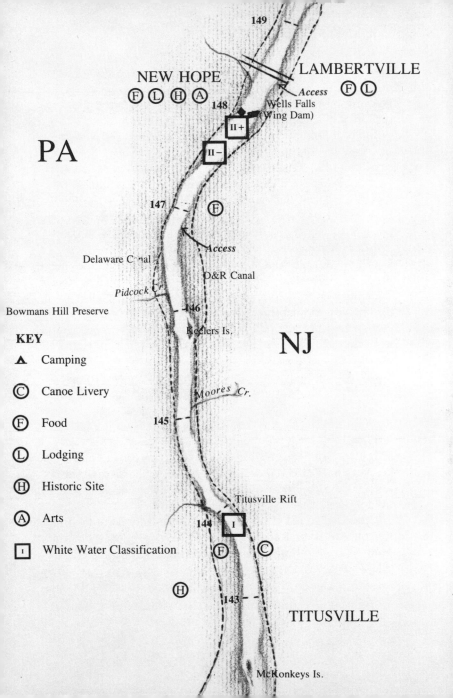

149

LAMBERTVILLE

NEW HOPE
(F) (L) (H) (A)   148
                                Access   (F) (L)
                          Wells Falls
                          (Wing Dam)

PA   II +

                    II −

          147   (F)

                        Access

Delaware C nal
                    D&R Canal

    Pidcock C

Bowmans Hill Preserve   146
                    Keelers Is.

KEY   NJ

▲ Camping

ⓒ Canoe Livery   *Moores Cr.*

Ⓕ Food   145

Ⓛ Lodging

Ⓗ Historic Site

Ⓐ Arts
                         Titusville Rift
☐ᵢ White Water Classification   144   ☐ I

                         (F)   (C)

                    (H)   143

                              TITUSVILLE

                    McKonkeys Is.

ville, New Jersey, and New Hope, Pennsylvania, see the features section of this chapter).

148.6–148.2. Shops, galleries, and restaurants of New Hope are close to water on Pennsylvania side.

148.6–148.5. The Lambertville access area extends about 100 yards along the New Jersey shore; powerboat ramp, limited parking, picnic tables, outhouses; operated by Delaware River Powerboat Association and D&R Canal State Park. There are many powerboats on river. Canoeists should stay near either shore.

148.1. Buoy advises "Falls ahead 200 feet."

148.0. Concrete wing dams extend from both sides to chute in the center of the river. Stop on either wing to reconnoiter—this is a potentially hazardous area. (See the description of Wells Falls in the features section of this chapter.)

Pass through chute into Wells Falls, a Class II + rapid with 3- to 4-foot standing waves and large rocks. After first drop, Class II rapids continue about 300 yards.

147.6. Rapids peter out into short eddy, with large rocks protruding from the water, Pennsylvania side.

146.8. Fireman's Eddy access area on New Jersey side; a gravel ramp constructed by New Jersey Young Adult Conservation Corps in 1980; emergency use only, closed to the general public.

The Golden Nugget Flea Market and Lambertville Flea Market, each with over 100 dealers of antiques and odds and ends for sale or trade, are located a short walk up New Jersey Route 29 from the access area.

The self-powered "Doodlebug," a single-car train of the Black River and Western Railroad, takes passengers for excursion rides from the Golden Nugget through the Hunterdon County countryside to Ringoes, New Jersey. From Ringoes passengers may change to a steam train to Flemington or return on the Doodlebug. The Black River and Western Railroad is a profitable short-line railroad.

146.2. Pidcock Creek enters, Pennsylvania side.

146.0. Keelers Island at New Jersey shore; left channel normally too dry for passage.

Bowmans Tower on hill, Pennsylvania side. (See description of Bowmans Hill in the features section of this chapter.)

145.1. Moores Creek enters, New Jersey side.

145.0. Belle Mountain Ski Area, New Jersey side.

144.1. River bends slightly left.

143.9. Enter Titusville Rift, Class I rapid, an unobstructed "V" through the bend with standing waves up to 1½ feet. Beware of shallows on the right.

143.1. The David Library of the American Revolution is across Route 32 on the Pennsylvania side. Open to the public.

143.0–142.0. Community of Titusville on bluffs, New Jersey side. Many docks, swimming rafts, and pontoon boats.

142.3. McKonkeys Island, Pennsylvania side. The channel along the Pennsylvania shore is impassable at low water.

142.0. Very mild riffle with a few exposed rocks. Washington Crossing State Parks, both sides; access not developed, but easy landing to picnic facilities, historic sites, etc. (See description of Washington's Crossing in the features section of this chapter).

141.8. Pass under Washington Crossing Bridge. A wooden bridge was built here in 1831, 55 years after Washington crossed in Durham boats. The present six-span steel truss bridge was completed in 1904 on the original masonry piers and abutments.

Enter Scudders Eddy; slow water for next mile.

140.5. Jacobs Creek enters, New Jersey side.

140.2. Goulds Island, Pennsylvania side. The right channel is too dry to canoe at low water.

139.7. Enter Scudders Falls, a Class I+ rapid. Concrete wing

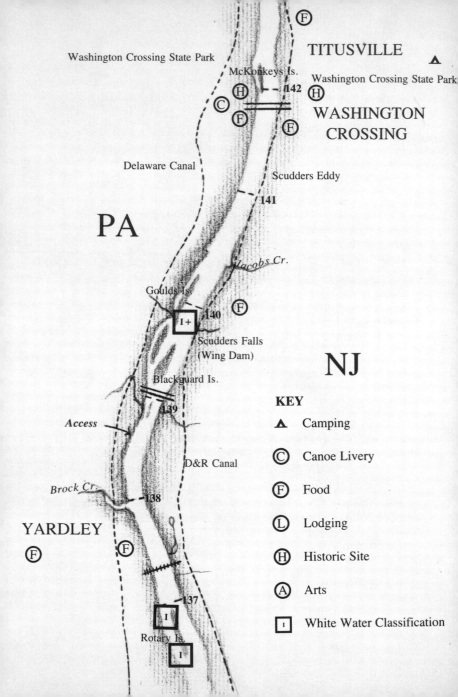

dams extend from both sides to chute at center. At normal level river does not flow over dams, but will when moderately high. *Do not canoe over dams* (dangerous hydraulic at foot of dams); *go through chute.* Passage through chute is an unobstructed "V." Standing waves about 2½ feet. "Only a drop and a rough race," in the words of J. Wallace Hoff.

A very narrow sluice at the extreme left (New Jersey side) provides a Class II rapid: waters drops along a concrete chute, breaks sharply right into two or three large standing waves, then returns to main channel. Very popular with kayakers from Mohawk Canoe Club, based on New Jersey shore just above Scudders Falls. Area below the dams is very popular with shad fishermen.

139.5. Blackguard Island in center of river; main channel is left, but right channel is navigable and accessible through a chute near the right end of the dam.

D&R Canal bends away from river and is no longer easily accessible.

139.1. Pass under Scudders Falls Bridge, carrying Interstate Route 95, completed in 1959.

139.0. Gravel bar in middle of channel.

138.7. Yardley public access area, Pennsylvania side. Offers a wide paved ramp, parking, outhouses, and trash deposit; maintained by Pennsylvania Fish Commission. This is the last public access before tidewater and the urbanized areas of Trenton.

138.0. Brock Creek enters, Pennsylvania side; may be followed a short distance to a canal aqueduct over the creek. Bridge abutment, Pennsylvania side, is all that remains of the old Yardley bridge, washed out in 1955 flood.

137.3. Brownstone abutments of an old Pennsylvania Railroad bridge.

The multiple-arch Conrail bridge carries the West Trenton line that runs between New York and Philadelphia. There is unimproved access under the bridge, Pennsylvania side.

137.0. Rotary Island (formerly Park Island) in center of the river: main channel is left, but right channel is passable and includes a stretch of Class I rapids with rocks and ledges at 136.6.

136.5. From left of island a channel winds through overhanging trees of Rotary Island; impassable at low water.

136.3. A Class I rapid immediately at the end of Rotary Island flows left to right.

136.1. A narrow island in center of river; submerged in moderately high water.

135.6–134.6. Holly Park, New Jersey side, parallels the river. There are playgrounds, picnic tables, and a physical fitness course. This park originally extended all the way to tidewater, but the lower reaches were obliterated, amid some controversy, with improvements to New Jersey Route 29.

134.6. Rocks protrude from water, Pennsylvania side; easy maneuvering.

134.4. Trenton City Waterworks intake, New Jersey side. Stay clear.

Pass under Calhoun Street Bridge. A wooden bridge was built here in 1861 but was destroyed later by fire. The present seven-span steel truss was completed on the original piers and abutments in 1884, making it the second-oldest bridge across the Delaware (the Roebling Bridge at Lackawaxen, built in 1849, is the oldest), and the oldest still used for vehicle traffic. There have been recent plans to build a new bridge nearby and to preserve the Calhoun Street Bridge as a historic site for use by pedestrians and bicyclists only.

134.1. Begin Trenton Falls, a Class I + rapid extending nearly one mile. The main channel is in the center of the river. Numerous rocks and ledges on right; impassable at normal water level.

Small island at extreme left (New Jersey side). In the channel to the left of island is a small dam with a narrow chute, canoeable

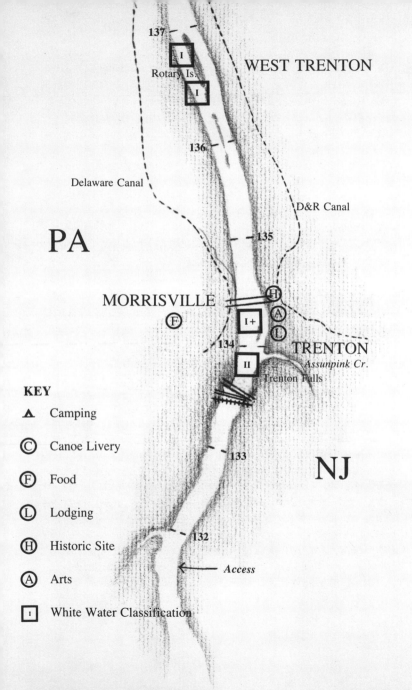

WEST TRENTON

137

I

Rotary Is.

I

136

Delaware Canal

D&R Canal

PA

135

MORRISVILLE

F

H

A

I+

L

134

TRENTON

Assunpink Cr.

II

Trenton Falls

133

NJ

132

Access

KEY

▲ Camping

ⓒ Canoe Livery

Ⓕ Food

Ⓛ Lodging

Ⓗ Historic Site

Ⓐ Arts

□ White Water Classification

but not recommended. Water crests the dam when moderately high, and the chute may be hard to see. Beware of hydraulic!

134.0. Upper limit of tidewater; if tide is high, the river is ponded from here down.

133.9. The gold dome of the New Jersey state capitol, New Jersey side. (See description of Trenton in features section of chapter).

133.8. Assunpink Creek enters, New Jersey side.

133.7. Ledges extend nearly across the river, as the main channel winds through the center. A maze of ledges on the right may be navigated with some lifting and dragging.

133.5. Pass under the Bridge Street Bridge, also known as the "Trenton Makes" bridge because of south-facing lettering proclaiming "Trenton Makes, the World Takes." The first span across the Delaware was built here in 1803–1806 upon the piers and abutments that now support the present bridge. The bridge structure itself was remodeled repeatedly, at one time carrying the railroad as well as vehicle traffic, until the present five-span steel truss was completed in 1930.

At extreme low tide Trenton Falls becomes a potentially hazardous Class II rapid with high standing waves and boulders under the bridge in middle-left of river. The rapid can be avoided by maneuvering as far right as possible.

133.4. Pass under U.S. Route 1 toll bridge, built in 1952. This marks the low tide limit.

133.3. Pass under the arched brownstone Amtrak mainline bridge, built in 1903. There is unimproved rough access under the bridge, Pennsylvania side.

133.2. Old Wharf fishing area, New Jersey side; operated by New Jersey Division of Fish, Game, and Shellfisheries. A wooden bulkhead with no boat access.

131.8. Mercer County public access area, primarily intended for access to tidal waters: concrete ramps, parking, trash disposal, and sanitary facilities.

FEATURES

New Hope, Pennsylvania

Located on the banks of the Delaware River, New Hope, Pennsylvania (population 1,473), is a small yet busy haven for artists, craftsmen, and tourists. It flourished as an industrial community in the nineteenth century; however, the big mills, no longer in operation, now stand vacant between the Delaware Canal and the river. New Hope today boasts 20 antique shops, four art galleries, nearly 100 specialty and gift shops, several night clubs (from sing-along piano bars to flashy discotheques), and more than 35 restaurants (from the Logan Inn founded in 1727 to Thomas Sweet's Ice Cream). There is an important regional theatre, barge rides on the Delaware Canal, a steam train to Lahaska, and historical tours.

New Hope was founded in the early 1700s by John Wells, who operated a ferry across the river and founded the Old Ferry Tavern, now known as the Logan Inn. The growing community became known as Coryells Ferry in honor of a subsequent ferry owner. In the late decades of the eighteenth century Benjamin Parry constructed and operated two mills which burned down in 1790. Parry rebuilt the mills and optimistically called them the "New Hope Mills." The name stuck, and the community itself soon became known as New Hope.

Virtually all of New Hope is within easy walking distance of the Delaware River. The entire town is squeezed onto four main streets, two alleys, and a towpath. The summer crowds are convivial, and the atmosphere day or night is captivating.

The city's special attractions are outlined below:

1. The Parry Mansion, at the corner of South Main and Ferry Streets, is open to the public during the summer to view the antique architecture, furnishings, and household items.
2. Mule barges take daily summer excursions 4½ miles along the Delaware Canal, departing hourly from the barge landing on the towpath just south of the center of town.
3. The Bucks County Playhouse, on South Main Street, features evening performances of well-known musicals.
4. Coryell's Ferry plies the Delaware River from its base between South Main Street and the riverbank.
5. The Lahaska Steam Railroad leaves several times a day from the depot near the canal at Bridge Street and tours 16 miles through the Bucks County countryside to Lahaska and back.
6. The Old Franklin Print Shop, at the corner of Ferry and South Main Streets features daily demonstrations of handpress printing.
7. The Antique Automobile Show and Flea Market, one of the largest of its type on the East Coast, is held the second weekend of every August.

Lambertville, New Jersey

Like New Hope on the other side of the river, Lambertville began as a ferry town, grew as a canal port, and burgeoned as a regional industrial center. Today, most of Lambertville's industry is gone, but the town is enjoying a renewal as a center of art, culture, and historical renovation.

The first permanent settler in Lambertville was one John Holcombe, who arrived in 1705. By 1770 Well's Ferry regularly plied between New Jersey and Pennsylvania. The little community became known as Coryells Ferry after 1770 when Emanuel Coryell superceded John Wells. (A restored "Coryell's Ferry" operates today out of New Hope as a tourist attraction.)

Lambertville acquired its present name in 1814 when John Lambert, a United States senator from New Jersey, arranged for his nephew's appointment as postmaster in the little village of 12 homes. With the construction of the Delaware and Raritan Canal in the 1830s and the Belvidere and Delaware Railroad in 1851, Lambertville developed into an important regional commercial center. Ample water power was available at Wells Falls, and mills were constructed for grist, paper, cotton, India rubber, saw timber, and iron works.

Just as railroads ultimately forced the closing of the D&R Canal, factories in the Midwest and in big eastern cities proved too fierce competition for the mills of Lambertville. Lambertville declined economically, and there has been little new construction since the turn of the century.

Today Lambertville is in a revival as a residential and cultural community. The citizens of Lambertville are proud of their heritage and actively promote historical preservation and restoration. Many of the old brick row houses have been renovated into modern artistic homes. Lambertville's Acme market has been featured in *Smithsonian Magazine* as a surviving example of art deco architecture. The long-abandoned railroad depot, built in 1880, has been recently reopened as a fine restaurant.

With a population of less than 5,000, Lambertville is not a large city. Yet many services and a variety of stores are available and easily accessible from the river. There are numerous cafes and restaurants, antique shops, boutiques, and grocery stores. The Lambertville House, a hotel-restaurant open to the public since 1812, stands just at the end of the Lambertville–New Hope Bridge. The restored Lambertville station restaurant is across the street. Lambertville's shops hold a sidewalk sale the last weekend of every July.

Wells Falls

There has always been a rapid at Wells Falls, which is named for the operator of an early ferry between Lambertville and New Hope. In 1812 wing dams were constructed to impound water for mill power, and so the river was confined to a narrow chute in the middle. The dam was upgraded most recently in 1968.

Wells Falls was one of the most difficult passages on the river for timber raftsmen in the eighteenth and nineteenth centuries. Local entrepreneurs familiar with the rapid made a good living by piloting rafts through Wells Falls at five dollars per raft. The pilots became so familiar with the passage that every rock was known to them by name: "100-barrel rock" (a Durham boat carrying 100 barrels of flour could pass when water covered this rock); "Foamer"; "Dram Rock"; "Buckwheat Ledge"; and "Rodmans Rocks," named for a raftsman who was wrecked and drowned at the site. The flow of the river has been so changed by the wing dams that the locations of these obstacles are known no longer.

A buoy half a mile downstream from the old New Hope–Lambertville Bridge warns "Danger—Falls ahead—200 feet." Wells Falls is indeed the most severe rapid on the Delaware River and is the only one measured above Class II by the DRBC. One warm summer day in 1981 the severity of the rapid was tragically proved.

On that day in 1981 the river level was normal, and flow was confined to the 25-foot wide chute between the wings. Half a dozen kayakers, wearing helmets and PFDs, challenged the wavefront breaking around the lip of the dam, trying to hold a stationary position on the wave, balancing current and gravity. People in rubber rafts bounced over and through the 3-foot haystacks where the river concentrates its momemtum just past the dam. Several canoeists stopped at the dam to reconnoiter their path through the rapids.

Then a lone canoe approached, bearing three passengers. They were going to go straight through, without stopping to learn the course. They wore no life jackets. The sternman sat not on the seat but high on the rear deck, sipping from a can of beer or soda. The circumstances were ripe for disaster.

The canoe sped through the chute, glanced off a rock, then rolled and swamped in the second haystack, pitching its occupants into the rapid. The three canoeists bobbed downriver, their boat, paddles, and persons separating in the rocks and crosscurrents. Some of the kayakers, seeing that the men were in trouble, paddled vigorously to the rescue. Two of the canoeists were pulled to safety, but the third could not be reached in time. His body was recovered by kayakers 15 minutes after the spill, and all attempts at reviving him were in vain. The hard lessons of river safety had been demonstrated once again.

Even for proficient canoeists Wells Falls represents a challenge. At normal water level, all the river rushes through the narrow chute between low wing dams extending from both banks. A great boulder, nearly submerged, lurks in the center of the chute just past the opening. The "V" of the main current flows to the right of the boulder, moving slightly left, with haystacks at least three feet high. A canoe almost certainly will take on several inches of water in a run of these waves, which makes for sluggish maneuvers around the rocks below. The actual channel is not more than ten feet wide.

It is possible to "sneak" Wells Falls at the extreme left side of the opening: the canoeist must make a very quick turn into the eddy behind the New Jersey wing, then negotiate between numerous small ledges and through narrow channels. This course is tricky, but the current is not so overwhelming as in the main channel.

When the river is high enough to flow over the dams, Wells Falls probably cannot be handled in an open canoe. The haystacks grow to four or five feet, and just submerged boulders hardly can be detected in the muddy flow. Canoeists should never attempt to go *over* the dams; the powerful hydraulic at the foot would easily trap a canoe and its occupants.

For those who believe that discretion is the better part of valor and determine that Wells Falls is beyond their capabilities, there are two very attractive alternatives. A canoe can be carried easily over either of the wing dams and placed into the eddy below; the route requires some maneuvering but avoids the severe current and waves encountered by passage through the chute. Or canoeists may portage a few yards to the D&R canal on the New Jersey bank, then paddle down the canal, and transfer back to the river below the falls.

As dangerous as it is, Wells Falls is an exciting challenge for intermediate canoeists. Safety precautions are essential: reconnoitering the route by stopping on either wing of the dam, securely fastening PFDs, and wearing helmets are advisable. After running the rapid, canoeists can beach on the New Jersey bank and haul their boats up to the D&R Canal. It is a fairly easy paddle back upstream to the Lambertville access area with a short portage around a lock.

Bowmans Hill

Any time during the spring, summer, and early fall wild flowers are plentiful all along the Delaware River. The riverside habitat is home to many species, and fields and forests just beyond the banks offer a niche to many more varieties. But at Bowmans Hill Wild Flower Preserve, part of Pennsylvania's Washington Crossing State Park about two miles south of New Hope, a score of different habitats have been established, providing visitors an opportunity to observe and study most of the common—and not so common—varieties of wild flowers found in this part of the country.

In the 1930s the Council for the Preservation of Natural Beauty sponsored the establishment of a wild flower preserve at the base of Bowmans Hill. In those early years volunteers and workers of the Works Progress Administration (WPA) cut trails, thinned undergrowth, drained and made swamps, and enhanced or established the range of habitats present today at the wild flower preserve. In the 1960s a headquarters was built to be used as an education and research center and to house collections and exhibits. Today the Bowmans Hill Wild Flower Preserve Association, together with the Pennsylvania State Park Service, continues to maintain and encourage the growth of wild flowers in the preserve.

Bowmans Hill Wild Flower Preserve is spread over a one hundred-acre tract along Pidcock Creek. More than 20 wild flower trails are arranged throughout the preserve: each takes the visitor through a different habitat and presents a different array of blossoms. Many of the trail habitats were present before the wild flower preserve was established; others were specially and carefully developed by importing soils, modifying moisture conditions, and varying exposures to sunlight.

Among the many habitats of Bowmans Hill Wild Flower Preserve is Penns Woods, where most of the species of trees native to Pennsylvania may be found. Visitors also may discover the barrens: habitats carefully established by importing rock and soil, supporting species indigenous to those peculiar conditions only. The marsh marigold trail, azaleas at the bridge, sphagnum, and the medicinal trail await exploration by visitors. These trails and 15 others each represent a different set of ecological niches.

The maintenance of Bowman Hill Wild Flower Preserve requires considerable expertise in the propagation and cultivation of plants that normally grow only in the wild and are often quite resistant to human interference. Wild plant propagation and cultivation are attempted constantly at the preserve, often with success but sometimes not. Wild plant propagation is a tricky business; each species has its own set of conditions that must be met before it can thrive. Very often these conditions are not known, so good guesswork and trial and error play a major role in the work at the wild flower preserve. Seed preparation, germination time (as much as four years!), amount and frequency of watering, temperature, acidity, nutrients, air supply, exposure to light, and soil all must be just so for wild flowers to prosper. The wild flower preserve has some excellent displays on wild plant propagation, and experiments may be seen throughout the preserve.

Throughout the year, but especially during the summer months, the wild flower preserve sponsors events for members of the association and for the public. On almost every summer Sunday there is a family nature walk: a guided tour of selected habitats of the preserve. Recently Wednesdays have been volunteer day; the public is invited to assist in the operation and maintenance of the preserve. This assistance might include collecting and sorting seeds, maintaining trails, and helping with the propagation of wild flowers. The preserve also sponsors special classes in horticulture and in wild flower propagation. A complete calendar of events is available from the preserve headquarters building. The headquarters building is open every day of the year, except major holidays, from 9:00 A.M. to 5:00 P.M. In addition to wild flower exhibits the headquarters building contains the Platt collection of bird nests, eggs, and mounted specimens.

The Wild Flower Preserve is not the only attraction of Bowmans Hill. At the summit of the hill stands Bowmans Hill Tower, erected in 1930. The spiral stairway to the top of the tower has been closed in recent years, but a new elevator is scheduled to be in operation by June, 1985. Bowmans Hill was used as an observation point by Washington's army in preparation for the Christmas night crossing in 1776. At the base of the hill and along the river are the Thompson-Neely House (built in 1702), the restored Thompson Gristmill, and the graves of Revolutionary soldiers.

Bowmans Hill is accessible from the river on the Pennsylvania side about one-half mile downstream from the Belle Mountain access area. Canoes may be landed near the mouth of Pidcock Creek at River Mile 146.2. A large picnic pavilion stands on the riverbank just upstream from Pidcock Creek.

Washington's Crossing

Washington's crossing of the Delaware on Christmas night in 1776 and the ensuing battle of Trenton reversed the direction of the American Revolution. Until then defeats and retreats had lowered the morale of the troops. Enlistments were over on December 31st, and most of the soldiers wanted to go home. The Revolutionary cause seemed hopeless.

Washington and a division of 2400 men were camped in the cold forest of Bucks County. A garrison of 1400 trained Hessian mercenaries was quartered eight miles downstream at Trenton.

Washington daringly planned a surprise attack on the Hessian garrison late on Christmas night; the Americans desperately needed this victory. Stealth was the essence of the operation. A spy named John Honeyman was employed by Washington to mingle with the Hessians at Trenton, to allow himself to be captured by the Americans, and to advise Washington of the enemy's activities. Daniel Bray, an officer in the Continental Army was charged with securing all the boats on the New Jersey side of the river. Bray assembled a small fleet of heavy Durham boats and flat-bottom ferries near the Pennsylvania shore. Without boats, the English army would not be able to pursue Washington across the river; and Bray's fleet, of course, played a critical role on the night of the attack.

Christmas night at Trenton was cold with blowing sleet and snow. The river was choked with an unusual amount of ice. From the Pennsylvania banks just upstream from the present Washington Crossing Bridge, the American soldiers poled and rowed to the New Jersey shore. The crossing took almost nine hours, much longer than Washington had planned. After the troops were assembled, Washington led a quick march eight miles to Trenton. The Hessians were completely surprised and conquered with few casualties. New hope had been breathed into the American cause.

The states of Pennsylvania and New Jersey have commemorated Washington's crossing of the Delaware by the establishment of two state parks. On the Pennsylvania side a group of Revolutionary-era homes, barns, and shops may be toured. McConkey's Ferry Inn, where Washington and his aides dined before the crossing, stands at the access to the bridge. The boat house shelters reproductions of the famous Durham boats, which were used during the crossing and to haul cargo along the Delaware River for many years. The highlight of a visit to Pennsylvania's Washington Crossing State Park is a reproduction of Emanuel Leutze's famous painting of Washington crossing the Delaware. The painting is located in a small theater within the visitors' center, and it is the focus of a narration describing the events of 1776. The visitors' center also houses other exhibits about the battle of Trenton and the Revolutionary War. There are two large picnic areas with pavilions and rest rooms.

Washington Crossing State Park, New Jersey, established in 1912, is considerably more extensive than its sister park across the river. There are at least four developed picnic areas with tables, pavilions, rest rooms, and grills, along with acres and acres of open space and shady spots for picnicking. Among the best of these spots is a grassy strip just atop the riverbank that extends several hundred yards upstream from the bridge. A new visitors' center, opened in 1976, features the Swan collection of the American Revolution. The Swan family has assembled an impressive display of Revolutionary firearms, swords, uniforms, letters, maps, money, and nearly every other artifact imaginable. An electric map and slide show tell the story of Washington's army in 1776. Curator Harry Swan is usually on hand.

Russell Hoover's remarkable painting of Washington crossing the Delaware is also on prominent display at the visitors' center. This painting, more historically accurate than the more famous work displayed in Pennsylvania, hung for many decades in a darkened stairwell in the Trenton Public Library before it was rediscovered in 1982.

Another feature of the park is the George Washington Memorial Arboretum, which contains more than 80 species of trees and shrubs. The New Jersey State Forest Nursery is also here, where many varieties of trees are propagated for planting on public and private lands throughout the state. There is also a nature center and natural area, a 7,000-foot-long physical fitness course, and numerous ballfields and play areas.

The Open Air Theater is one of the highlights of New Jersey's Washington Crossing State Park. Sponsored by the Washington Crossing Association of New Jersey, local theater groups perform on a grand stage in the center of a natural amphitheater. There is a performance almost every night in the summer, and admission is reasonable.

The park makes its facilities available throughout the year for special events like the antique gasoline engine show every September 17th and 18th. The community of Titusville sponsors a fireworks display over the river around the Fourth of July.

Washington's crossing of the Delaware is re-enacted, complete with troops in Revolutionary uniforms and Durham boats, every Christmas afternoon. Thousands and thousands of people line the bridge and New Jersey and Pennsylvania banks to witness and participate in this annual event.

Washington Crossing State Park is accessible from the river on either shore immediately upstream from the Washington Crossing Bridge. All park facilities are within walking distance of the river. The shoreline itself is gradual and makes for easy landing, but the banks are high and steep. Access is not developed.

Trenton, New Jersey

The sign on the bridge between Trenton and Morrisville boldly states, "Trenton Makes, the World Takes." Trenton, New Jersey, population 92,124, has long been an important manufacturing center. One of its earliest manufactures was ceramics, and this continues to be an important industry in Trenton, where Lenox fine china and American Standard plumbing fixtures are head-

Trenton. The capital city of New Jersey seen from the Calhoun Street Bridge just after sunrise. Trenton Falls and the upper limit of tidewater are just downstream. The Calhoun Street Bridge, completed in 1884, is the oldest span still in use across the Delaware. Photo by the author.

quartered. Roebling Steel began manufacturing wire cables for suspension bridges in Trenton in 1848, and the Roebling Company remains there today. Other plants in Trenton produce rubber goods, fabrics, electrical parts, and other commodities.

In 1679 Quaker Mahlon Stacy built a house and gristmill at "Ye Ffalles of Ye De La Warr." William Trent, a merchant from Philadelphia, purchased some of Stacy's land and divided it for sale in 1714. "Trent's town" grew as it attracted commerce from the upper Delaware. In 1727 a ferry across the river began operations to convey passengers on their way between New York City and Philadelphia, and in 1806 the first permanent bridge to span the Delaware was constructed at the head of tidewater in Trenton.

The modern Bridge Street Bridge, with its "Trenton Makes" sign, stands on the original piers and abutments.

One of the most important battles of the Revolutionary War was fought in Trenton, when on Christmas night 1776 George Washington led his troops to capture the Hessian garrison. Although the United States Congress met in Trenton in 1784, attempts to make Trenton the capital of the new nation were unsuccessful.

Trenton is the capital of New Jersey. The gold dome of the statehouse is clearly visible from the Delaware River. Other government buildings are clustered in the capital complex that rises above the river, including Labor and Industry, Health and Agriculture, and the new Richard Hughes Justice Center.

There are numerous historic buildings and sites in Trenton, most of them easily accessible from the Delaware River. William Trent's home, built in 1719, is open as a museum not far from the Bridge Street Bridge. The Old Barracks, built in 1758, housed many of the Hessian officers captured in Washington's raid. The Old Barracks is open as a museum and may be found just below the statehouse. Across the street is the old Masonic lodge, built in 1793.

The state library, the state museum, and the domed planetarium are located close to the river just below the Calhoun Street Bridge. The museum contains fascinating permanent exhibits of the natural and cultural history of New Jersey. Special art exhibits change every few months. The planetarium has several shows daily.

As an old industrial city, parts of Trenton have fallen into urban decay. But the community is making great efforts to refurbish these areas, and citizens of Trenton are proud of their heritage. The whole city turns out for the annual heritage days festival, held during the first weekend of June, for a smorgasbord of activities, arts and crafts, and ethnic foods.

There are, of course, many stores and services available in Trenton, but for the most part these are not near to the Delaware River. Canoeists seeking supplies are advised to look in Morrisville, Pennsylvania, near the Calhoun Street and Bridge Street crossings.

CAMPING AND SERVICES

Camping

There are no public or private campgrounds for canoeists along this section of the river. At Washington Crossing State Park, New Jersey, there is a group campsite about ½ mile from the river. Most of the land along the river here is either farmland or built upon. The river islands are owned privately, and permission must be secured before camping.

Canoe Livery

1. Abbott's Canoe Rental (Route 29, Titusville, New Jersey 08650, 609/737–3446), River Mile 143.5, is located about 2 miles north of Washington Crossing Bridge on New Jersey Route 29. Abbott's has about 80 canoes available for day rental on the D&R Canal or the Delaware River. Reservations in advance are necessary for portage. For something different, Abbott's rents pedal boats on the D&R Canal.
2. George's Canoe Rental (Route 532, Washington Crossing, Pennsylvania 18977, 215/493–2366) is located on the Delaware Canal where it is crossed by Pennsylvania Route 532, about ½ mile inland from Washington Crossing Bridge.

George's features canoes, kayaks, and pedal boats for use
on the Delaware Canal.

Other Services

Services found within the communities of New Hope, Lambertville, and Trenton are more fully discussed in the features section of this chapter. Other services available in this section are
listed below:

147.2 Lambertville, New Jersey. Golden Nugget Restaurant,
associated with the Golden Nugget flea market. Access from Belle
Mountain access area.

143.8 Washington Crossing, Pennsylvania. Fife and Drum
Restaurant, lunch available on patio tables.

142.6 Titusville, New Jersey. Huber's Soft Ice Cream Stand.

141.8 Washington Crossing, New Jersey. Paronni's Deli,
featuring sandwiches, ice cream, coffee to go, and snacks, is located at the New Jersey end of Washington Crossing Bridge. A
pay phone is available. Faherty's Pub is in this same building.

141.8 Washington Crossing, Pennsylvania. Sandwiches to go
are available in the little market at the access to Washington Crossing Bridge. A pizzeria, drug store, and post office are in a little
shopping center about ¼ mile from the bridge on Pennsylvania
Route 532. The grand old Washington Crossing Inn is at the intersection of Routes 32 and 532.

140.0 Washington Crossing, New Jersey. Landwehrs Restaurant, fine dining.

137.9 Yardley, Pennsylvania. Charcoal Steaks and Things,
snack bar and dining room. Food may be carried out to the picnic
tables on the riverbank. There is a good canoe landing immediately downstream from the abutments of the old Yardley Bridge.

137.8 Yardley, Pennsylvania. This community has many services available within easy walking distance of the river. The Yardley Inn stands at the old Yardley Bridge abutment. On Main Street restaurant service is available at the Continental Tavern, Vince's Pizza, Mary Ann's kitchen, and Yardley Pharmacy. There is a U.S. Post Office, supermarket, laundromat, Fotomat, bakery, two pharmacies, J.D. Sachs outdoors store, Wawa quick-mart, and the Old Yardley Gristmill, now developed as a mini-mall.

Appendix
Quick Guide to
the Delaware River

I PUBLIC ACCESS

	Mile
1. Balls Eddy (West Branch, PA)	**335.3**
2. Buckingham (PA)	**325.1**
3. Equinunk (PA)	**323.0**
4. Callicoon (NY)	**303.6**
5. Callicoon (PA)	**303.1**
6. Cochecton (NY)	**298.5**
7. Damascus (PA)	**298.3**
8. Skinners Falls (NY)	**295.4**
9. Narrowsburg (NY)	**290.1**
10. Narrowsburg (PA)	**289.9**
11. Lackawaxen (PA)	**277.6**
12. Matamoras (PA)	**256.1**
13. Milford (PA)	**246.2**
14. Dingmans Ferry (PA)	**238.5**
15. Eshbeck (PA)	**231.6**
16. Bushkill (PA)	**228.2**
17. Depew Island (NJ)	**221.3**
18. Pahaquarry (NJ)	**220.0**
19. Smithfield Beach (PA)	**218.0**
20. Worthington State Forest (NJ)	**214.6**
21. Kittatinny (NJ)	**211.7**
22. Metropolitan Edison (PA)	**206.7**
23. Martins Creek (PA)	**194.2**

24.	Sandts Eddy (PA)	**189.9**
25.	Frost Hollow Park (PA)	**186.5**
26.	Eddyside Park (PA)	**185.0**
27.	Easton Beach (PA)	**184.4**
28.	Phillipsburg (NJ)	**184.0**
29.	Easton Front Street (PA)	**183.7**
30.	Fry's Run Park (PA)	**176.7**
31.	Rieglesville (NJ)	**174.6**
32.	Holland Church (NJ)	**173.7**
33.	Upper Black Eddy (PA)	**167.7**
34.	Kingman (NJ)	**163.4**
35.	Tinicum County Park (PA)	**162.9**
36.	Byron (NJ)	**156.1**
37.	Bulls Island (NJ)	**155.3**
38.	Lambertville (NJ)	**148.6**
39.	Belle Mountain (NJ)	**146.8**
40.	Yardley (PA)	**138.7**
41.	Mercer County (NJ)	**131.8**

II RAPIDS (I + OR MORE)

1.	Long Eddy I +	**315.0**
2.	Hankins I +	**310.9**
3.	Skinners Falls II	**295.2**
4.	(unnamed) I +	**286.6**
5.	Ten-Mile Rift II −	**285.0**
6.	West Colang Rift II	**281.4**
7.	Narrows Falls Rift II −	**279.4**
8.	Big Cedar Rift II −	**275.0**
9.	Shohola Rift II	**272.9**
10.	Buttermilk Falls I +	**270.5**

11. (unnamed) I+ — **266.7**
12. Stairway Rift I+ — **263.3**
13. Mongaup Falls II− — **261.0**
14. Butlers Falls I+ — **260.0**
15. Sawmill Rift I+ — **258.7**
16. Quicks Rift I+ — **248.8**
17. Mary and Sambo Rift I+ — **224.6**
18. Stony Brook Rift I+ — **209.0**
19. (unnamed) I+ — **205.2**
20. Buttermilk Rift I+ — **199.3**
21. Foul Rift II — **196.7**
22. Capush Rift I+ — **194.9**
23. Hog Rift I+ — **186.5**
24. Rieglesville Rift I+ — **174.6**
25. (unnamed) I+ — **170.1–169.9**
26. Lott Falls I+ — **158.3**
27. Lumberville Wing Dams I+ — **155.9**
28. Wells Falls II+ — **148.0**
29. Scudders Falls I+ — **139.7**
30. Trenton Falls I+ — **134.1**
31. Trenton Falls (low tide) II — **133.5**

III GEOLOGIC INTEREST

1. Point Mountain (Hancock) — **330.7**
2. Skinners Falls (Milanville) — **295.2**
3. Hawks Nest Mountain (Sparrowbush) — **260.0**
4. Sawkill Falls (Milford) — **246.2**
5. Walpack Bend (Bushkill) — **226.7**
6. Delaware Water Gap — **212.1**
7. Slateford Farm Quarry (Delaware Water Gap) — **209.5**

  8. Terminal Moraine (Belvidere)   **201.0**
  9. Foul Rift (Belvidere)   **196.7**
10. Palisades of the Delaware (Rieglesville)   **171.9**
11. Ringing Rocks (Upper Black Eddy)   **169.0**
12. New Jersey State Museum (Trenton)   **134.4**
13. Trenton Falls   **133.5**

IV HISTORY

  1. Fort Delaware (Narrowsburg)   **290.2**
  2. Roebling Bridge (Lackawaxen)   **277.4**
  3. Battle of Minisink (Minisink Ford)   **277.3**
  4. Erie Depot (Port Jervis)   **254.7**
  5. Fort Decker (Port Jervis)   **254.7**
  6. Pike County Historical Museum (Milford)   **246.1**
  7. Pinchot Institute (Milford)   **246.1**
  8. Old Mine Road (Flatbrookville)   **233.5**
  9. Millbrook Village   **223.5**
10. Slateford Farm (Delaware Water Gap)   **209.5**
11. Easton Walking Tour   **183.7**
12. Hugh Moore Canal Museum (Easton)   **183.6**
13. Delaware Canal   **183.6–134.5**
14. Route 32 Inns   **168.0–148.8**
15. Irwin Stover House (Erwinna)   **162.8**
16. Delaware and Raritan Canal   **156.0–139.5**
17. David Library of the Revolution
      (Washington Crossing)   **143.1**
18. Washington Crossing   **141.8**
19. New Jersey State Museum (Trenton)   **134.4**
20. City of Trenton   **133.5**

V ARTS

1. Delaware Arts Alliance (Narrowsburg)	**290.0**
2. Zane Grey Museum (Lackawaxen)	**277.6**
3. Peters Valley Crafts Village	**(238.5)**
4. Walpack Arts Center	**(232.0)**
5. Watergate Recreation Area Concerts	**221.3**
6. Shawnee Playhouse (Shawnee-on-Delaware)	**214.7**
7. Hugh Moore Canal Museum (Easton)	**183.6**
8. Stover Mill (Erwinna)	**162.3**
9. Bucks County Playhouse (New Hope)	**148.3**
10. Lambertville Flea Markets	**146.7**
11. Washington Crossing Theatre	**142.0**
12. New Jersey State Museum (Trenton)	**134.4**

VI ACTIVITIES AND FESTIVALS

1. Dash and Splash Race (first weekend in May) (Narrowsburg)	**290.1**
2. Narrowsburg Fireworks (July 4)	**290.0**
3. Bluegrass Festival (TBA) (Barryville)	**275.0**
4. Canoe Regatta (Memorial Day) (Port Jervis)	**254.7**
5. Peters Valley Crafts Fair (last weekend in July)	**(238.5)**
6. Easton Shad Tournament (April 20–May 5)	**183.7**
7. Easton Farmers' Market (Tuesdays, Thursdays, Saturdays)	**183.7**
8. New Hope Antique Auto Show	**148.5**
9. Lahaska Steam Train (New Hope)	**148.5**
10. Black River and Western Railroad (Lambertville)	**146.7**
11. Washington's Crossing Re-enactment (Christmas)	**141.7**
12. Titusville Fireworks (July 5)	**141.7**
13. Trenton Heritage Days (first weekend in June)	**133.5**

Glossary

Eddy: A current running contrary to the direction of the main current, often found on the downstream side of an obstacle. Also, a long slow stretch of river.

Eskimo roll: A kayaking technique in which the kayaker rights himself from a submerged head-down position.

Haystacks: Stationary waves caused by forceful flow of water through a clear channel. Also known as standing waves.

Hydraulic: The turbulent, usually circular flow of water at the foot of a ledge or obstruction.

Livery: A concern offering canoes and canoeing equipment for rent.

Ponded or pooled: Describes still or very slow-moving water, often held back by a dam or natural feature.

Portage: Overland transport of canoes or equipment between different points on a river.

Riffle: Fast, rippling water over a shallow bottom.

Rift: Fast water or rapids, often separating stretches of slow water or eddies.

Tidewater: Portions of the river that rise and fall with the tide.

Wing dam: A low dam with a gap at the center of the river.

Bibliography

Beck, Henry Charlton. *Tales and Towns of Northern New Jersey*. New Brunswick, New Jersey: Rutgers University Press, 1964.

Bowmans Hill Wild Flower Preserve Association. *Ways with Wild Flowers*. New Hope, Pennsylvania: Bowmans Hill Wild Flower Preserve Association, 1983.

Corbett, Roger, and Fulcomer, Kathleen. *The Delaware River*. Springfield, Virginia: Seneca Press, 1981.

Delaware and Raritan Canal Commission. *Delaware and Raritan Canal State Park Master Plan*. Trenton, New Jersey, 1977.

Fisher, Ronald M. *The Appalachian Trail*. Washington, D.C.: National Geographic Society, 1972.

Henn, William F. *Westfall Township, Gateway to the West*. Milford, Pennsylvania: Pike County Historical Society, 1978.

Life Along the Delaware from Bushkill to Milford. Milford, Pennsylvania: Pike County Historical Society, 1975.

Hine, Charles Gilbert. *The Old Mine Road*. New Brunswick, New Jersey: Rutgers University Press, 1963.

Hoff, J. Wallace. *Two Hundred Miles on the Delaware*. Trenton, New Jersey: The Brandt Press, 1893.

Hungerford, Edward. *Men of Erie*. New York: Random House, 1946.

Kraft, Herbert C. *The Archeology of the Tocks Island Area*. South Orange, New Jersey: Seton Hall University Museum, 1975.

McPhee, John. *In Suspect Terrain*. New York: Farrar, Strauss, Giroux, 1982.

New York–New Jersey Trail Conference. *New York Walk Book*. Garden City, New York: Doubleday/Natural History Press, 1971.

Punola, John A. *Canoeing and Fishing the Upper Delaware River*. Madison, New Jersey: Pathfinder Publications, 1979.

Riviere, Bill. *Pole, Paddle, and Portage*. New York: Van Nostrand Reinhold Co., 1969.

Rivinus, Willis M. *A Wayfarer's Guide to the Delaware Canal*. Willis M. Rivinus, 1964.

Wakefield, Manville B. *Coal Boats to Tidewater*. South Fallsburg, New York: Manville B. Wakefield, 1965.

Weiss, Harry B. *Rafting on the Delaware River*. Trenton, New Jersey: New Jersey Agricultural Society, 1967.

Weslager, Clinton Alfred. *The Delaware Indians*. New Brunswick, New Jersey: Rutgers University Press, 1972.

Widmer, Kemball. *The Geology and Geography of New Jersey*. Princeton, New Jersey: D. Van Nostrand Co., 1964.